Copyright

M000210773

No part of this book may be reproduced, or stored in a retrieval system, or transmitted in any form or by any means, electronic, mechanical, photocopying, recording, or otherwise, without express written permission of the publisher.

Moral Rights: William "King" Hollis asserts the moral right to be identified as the author of this work.

External Content: William "King" Hollis has no responsibility for the persistence or accuracy of URLs for external or third-party Internet Websites referred to in this publication and does not guarantee that any content on such Websites is, or will remain, accurate or appropriate.

Designations: Designations used by companies to distinguish their products are often claimed as trademarks. All brand names and product names used in this book and on its cover are trade names, service marks, trademarks and registered trademarks of their respective owners. The publishers and the book are not associated with any product or vendor mentioned in this book. None of the companies referenced within the book have endorsed the book.

ISBN-13: 9780578767321

Printed in the United States of America

THE BEST GIFTS COME FROM THE BOTTOM

Kings' starter guide to a successful career
in motivational speaking.

By

William "King" Hollis

SPECIAL THANKS

I want to express a very special Thank You to all of my guardian angels, the ones who helped me push through, the ones that encouraged me along the way, the ones who believed in my gift and mission. To Bebe, Shawlanda Jones, Dartangyala White, Bonne Dutton, Delvin Sullivan, Sam Rogers, Bernie Nowatarski, Kenneth Biz Stevens, Kelvin Powell, Butter Bill and Joey Wilcoxson, words can not express the full gratitude I have for you all. Thank You!

-William King Hollis

TABLE OF CONTENTS

FORWARD

Every now and then there is someone in our history that achieves greatness even when the odds may seem against them. They rise above the criticism and all the people that seemed to have given up on the possibility of their success. When they rise, they accomplish things that nobody ever thought were possible. That is exactly what William Hollis has done in a very short period of time and at a young age. If you look at statistics, William wasn't supposed to make it. Having a father in prison and a loving mother who unfortunately battled with drugs, the world constantly told him that he would never make it out of his environment. He knew he was meant for more and didn't allow anything or anyone to stop him from believing that. William is someone who truly tapped into his greatest gift which is his ability to transform and inspire people with just the sound of his voice. He spoke himself out of homelessness and is now one of the upcoming top speakers of his generation. I marvel at his drive, his perseverance, and his desire to make a difference in the lives of so many others. His presence on the stage commands your attention from America to many countries around the world. Learn all that you can from this book and know that you too can live your dreams. Your circumstances do not predict your story and you have the power to change your direction at any time.

William Hollis is truly an example of exactly what happens when you believe in yourself, embrace your gifts, and you never quit. I call him a son because in many ways he reminds me of my younger self. Passionate, full of life, and always prepared to help his fellow man . I call him a friend because of his love, generosity and kindness. May William and the pages of this book bring you the prosperity, motivation, and the true belief that absolutely anything is possible in your life.

Les Brown

INTRODUCTION

Having a career as a motivational speaker can be incredibly rewarding. You can help others through tough situations, teach others, acquire financial stability, and even learn throughout the entire process. You can also inspire others to find passions similar to yourself, and breed a whole new generation of people with a hunger for learning. If you believe that you have a gift that could give others something positive in their life, then you may want to consider how beneficial a career as a motivational speaker could be.

Are you an executive who wants to break away from the corporate world and speak to audiences around the globe? Do you have a story to tell that others would pay to listen to? Is being a motivational speaker your next career opportunity?

The ultimate goal of a motivational speaker is to change people profoundly on an emotional and/or mental level, and to help them make some kind of professional or personal change in their lives and within themselves. People naturally tend to focus on all their problems, and the motivational speaker will help an audience to focus on the many opportunities instead, by using any number of persuasive speech tactics to inspire and motivate.

Some speakers may be hired to speak as special guests, and others travel a planned circuit of speaking engagements. The more popular motivational speakers may also write and sell inspirational books, dvd's and appear on television.

Almost all motivational speakers relate their own personal experience to an audience, which means they can come from any kind of background and use that information to inspire others. Not everyone evaluates their significant life experiences to determine if those experiences could be helpful to others. A motivational speaker is constantly reflecting on their own life to see what information would be helpful to their audiences or clients. They speak in a variety of venues like schools, company boardrooms, community centres, and conferences.

There are a few motivational speakers within different areas of expertise:

Personal Development

This is the type of speaker that is most commonly thought of when "motivational speaker" is mentioned. They inspire and guide listeners to find purpose and meaning in their life. They may give talks on motivation, inspiration, or overcoming adversity, which in turn helps people to take action and see the world or their situation from a new perspective.

Business

These types of speakers provide encouragement and guidance to business teams at varying levels, from sales people to executive directors. Business speakers usually have experience in business and are able to share their own stories of success (and failure). They cultivate enthusiasm, help teams develop a common purpose, and inspire them to improve their work.

Youth Mentor

The goal of a youth mentor is to give kids some positive guidance and a sense of direction in their formative years. They hope to inspire young people to lead healthy, ambitious lives, which may include topics like taking school seriously, finding their calling in life, studying hard, and learning how to interact with others in a healthy way. They may address young people at schools, churches, community centres, and a variety of other venues.

Community

These types of speakers give motivational talks about important social and community issues. Their goal is to educate the public and give them the power to take positive action, or they may give a speech that rallies people together for a good cause.

Motivational speakers build successful careers from life experiences. They share their powerful messages with others who benefit from the wisdom gained by those experiences. In this article, we discuss what a motivational speaker is, why they're important, how to become one, and the skills you need to be successful. You will also learn how you can transition from having a genuine passion to becoming a professional public speaker who inspires others.

Think of the many times you found yourself in a crowd, listening to some stranger speaking eloquently and confidently to the crowd. Can you remember how you felt during those times, particularly how the words of the speaker affected you? Did their words even have an impact on you, even in a small way?

More importantly, when it was all over, what did you take away from the experience? What did you learn, and what action did you take that was spurred by what the speaker said?

As much as we put a lot of stock on the things we read about in the papers or online, the spoken word still tends to have more impact. We hear something, we tend to believe it more than what we read on print. This is why motivational speakers are getting more recognition nowadays, because of the "power" and influence that they wield with their words, and how they deliver them.

Many people get started on the path of becoming a motivational speaker mainly because they want to inspire people with their strong speeches. I mean, who wouldn't want to be considered an inspirational rockstar?

Without a doubt, motivational speakers play a huge role not only in inspiring people, but also in communicating important academic and political insights that can benefit society. This is probably why so many people consider becoming one. But, becoming one is not as easy at it looks. If fact, motivational speaking is one of the most challenging jobs in the world today, which is exactly why professional speakers get paid the big bucks.

Now, there are people like Tony Robbins and the late, great Zig Ziglar who I classify as traditional motivational speakers. These gurus have helped their audiences reach new levels of success and much more. They focus on achieving personal and professional goals, breaking through barriers and being better than you ever thought possible. They motivate you to action, just like any good speaker in any subject must do. In the case of the Tony Robbins-type of speaker, the term "motivational speaker" is as much a title as it is a description of what they do.

I bring all of this up because over the years I've been asked by many people how to become a motivational speaker. The term "motivational speaker" has become a generic term to describe a professional speaker. What they really mean is that they want to be paid to speak in front of an audience. Some of these people are high-level executives who are looking to leave the corporate world and want to share their knowledge as they wind down their professional careers. Others are looking to break away from traditional employment. To them, the idea of being paid to speak is appealing. Some people have a story or passion and a yearning to share it with others.

MOTIVATIONAL SPEAKING OVER SUICIDE (WILLIAM "KING" HOLLIS)

I learned how to face adversity and work through suicidal depression at an early age, due to a heroin-addicted mother and incarcerated father. With over 400 million views on YouTube, at 31-years-old I am able to motivate millions of people on different platforms all across the world; speaking hope, courage and motivation into those who feel like giving up on their goals, dreams, and their life.

I am best known for my football speech, "The Game of Life". I became internationally recognized as the first motivational speaker to perform during Milan Fashion Week in front of 30,000 people, headlining the premiere of the luxury sports line, Plein Sports, for Philipp Plein in Milan, Italy. I literally made history and walked away with $10,000 after a four minute speech. With all that said, the speech that holds a special place in my heart, the ground zero of my career, and is my pride is a speech given to 5 teenagers at Reading Intermediate High School in Reading, Pennsylvania.

You see, my childhood was a constant battle of trying to save my mothers' life from heroin. With the stress, pain, and responsibility on my shoulders at home, I never allowed my home life to be discussed at school, for fear of being taken away from my mother. I knew at a very young age if I told anyone about my mother I was going to be taken away. Although I ended up not being taken away, I never had stability as I bounced back and forth between my mother and grandmother. I dealt with things no kid should ever have to deal with, but knowing I had to do something to save my mother I kept grinding through life and used my ability in sports to deal with anger management and it became the vehicle to keep driving toward that goal.

Not being able to read until I was 16-years-old, but being an absolute beast on the football field, I knew enough that my high school coaches and college scouts were more concerned with and excited about how good I could play football and not my inability to read. I just went to class and did the minimum and they knew about my IEP (Individual Education Plan). Some teachers just felt sorry for me and passed me along.

After graduating from Alexander Hamilton High School in Los Angeles, California, I went on to play football at the next level in college. I played for a couple of community colleges and then ended up with a scholarship to Clark Atlanta University, a chance to be really seen. I had a mission, a goal of saving my mother and nothing was going to get in my way. When I suited up for every game I didn't play the game, I lived it. Every player that was put in front of me was another obstacle between me and saving my mother so I never held back, I pushed myself to the extreme. Even with a football scholarship, I had difficulties through college. Maintaining focus on my mission, dealing with other distractions in life and having a learning disability I continued to struggle with fighting and pushing forward to reach my goal of saving my mother.

Looking to regain focus, I received a call and try-out offer that ended up turning into a full scholarship to continue playing football at the University of North Alabama. A new opportunity, a bigger platform, I knew this was one step closer to being able to save my mother. Just as I was preparing for the upcoming season at North Alabama, my fiance, the mother of my daughter Halo, called and let me know her mother was in a paralyzing vehicle accident. We both now had mothers that needed our help and a daughter that was going to get caught in between. I knew then I had to make a choice, keep grinding toward my goal to save my mother or go up to Boston and be the father I never had to support my family. I went up to Boston, depressed knowing that I was so close to my goal, but also humbled and grateful to God for giving me a beautiful family to take care of. I went and worked for a hospital in Boston, while still holding on to the dream of finishing out my mission to save my mother and now to take care of my family.

Struggling internally both mentally and emotionally, I continued to hold onto the dream and goal of saving my mother. Even though things on the outside were looking on the up and up, I was still battling inside myself. I received a glimmer of hope one day when a former coach of mine called me up to check in. He gave me an opportunity to try-out in an open camp at Tuskegee University.

Before going to the try-out, out of shape, I headed out to California to hook up with my cousin and a couple of NFL greats to get myself back to being football ready. Two weeks into the training I was feeling great....and then... I got the phone call that my mother, my best friend, my reason for grinding through all of the pain was found dead from a heroin overdose in a drug house back home. This broke me down, but I knew in my heart after the air cleared that I had to finish what I started. I needed to seize the opportunity that was given to me, now not for my mother but for me. My mother's funeral was the first place I ever gave any kind of speech, that speech has stuck with me through today.

Wanting football to heal the brokenness, and believing that I had to continue on striving to complete the mission through football, I approached the game with a relentless mentality and pressed on, with a duffle bag of clothes, no money, no food, and no plans of where I was going to sleep, I went to the try-out at Tuskegee University. By sheer determination and a hunger that wasn't going to let anyone outperform me, I made the team. I only spent 1 year at Tuskegee University, then moved on to other professional try-outs, teams, and ended up playing professional indoor football. Climbing a bit out of the funk of depression while still living with the pain of loss of my mother, I found it in myself to continue grinding through the game of football.

I got myself to the point I was set, categorized as a "Top 25 Defensive Lineman" in the nation and an NFL prospect, my goal was in arms reach, I could almost touch it...and then... I didn't realize, but I had pushed myself so hard I cracked a vertebrae in my back. This injury shattered my hopes of playing professional football and would keep me from ever living up to the goals and mission I had set for myself.

I truly hit rock bottom, and I had become homeless there in Reading, Pennsylvania. I was having suicidal thoughts and had a 45. pistol in my hotel room ready to end my life when God sent me someone. I was inside this Turkey Hill Gas Station and a lady that had seen me speak to kids at a local school during an outreach program with the football team came and asked if I would come speak at Reading Intermediate High School. Not knowing what to expect and just wanting to go show some love to these kids, little did I know my life was about to change. I went into that school and spoke to 5 teenagers. Within 5 minutes of me speaking they were all emotionally touched and tears began to roll down their faces at the words that were coming out of mouth.

After speaking to that small group of kids and realizing I wasn't just talking to them but I was talking to myself too, it saved me from committing suicide. It was like a phone call from God putting me into a motivational mode, and letting me know that the answers are inside of me, and inside of you. God put a mission on my heart to motivate and wake-up the souls of people that are dying inside because of depression, stress, all types of mental health and pain, along with those who struggle with self image and life as a whole.

That day as I walked out of that high school, the superintendent stopped me and asked me how much I charge, this became the turning point for me and gave me a newly defined purpose and recognition of a gift I was meant to share to the world.

You see, when we are given a gift but are drowning from suicidal thoughts, depression, and pains in this life, we often can't fathom that we are worth anything to anyone and we can't see through the fog the value within ourselves to have anything to offer this world. I'm not that motivator that's going to tell you, oh, you have greatness in you. I'm going to tell you; it's going to be painful. If you're not willing to work through pain, not willing to work through life's tragedies, you will never be able to see the King or Queen that you are.

In my speeches and my coaching I always look to the

inner King and Queen in everyone I engage with. I use my family and life experiences to connect with those who have dealt with and continue to deal with similar trials. My inspiration is drawn from accepting what God has allowed me to go through in this life.

From Reading, Pennsylvania to Milan, Italy along with a number of other states and countries, I have continuously chose motivational speaking over suicide. The thoughts of my daughters give me renewed strength to push on. After spending my life trying to save my mother's life, I know now the significance and power of words that can change and even save someone's life.

MOTIVATIONAL SPEAKING

When we hear about motivational speakers, more often than not, our minds immediately picture someone who is very inspirational, talking about very serious topics, mostly self-help. However, that is a narrow way of looking at it, because motivational speaking is not something that only self-help gurus and personalities have a monopoly on.

Motivational speaking can be about any topic under the sun. It can even be about something as trivial as choosing what to wear for the day. What sets motivational speaking apart from other types of public speaking is the passion that goes into it, specifically the passion for the subject matter.

We can name four essentials of motivational speaking:

• The message or the subject matter or the topic that will be delivered to the audience;

• The audience or the recipient of the message. These are the people that the speaker aims to motivate;

• The speaking skills of the motivational speaker or his public speaking abilities, specifically how he delivers the message through speeches and presentations; and

• The passion of the motivational speaker to convey his message to audience.

All four must be present when it comes to motivational speaking.

THE MOTIVATIONAL SPEAKER

Here is a question in many people's minds: Can anyone become a motivational speaker?

Before I can give an answer to that, let us first get to know the "motivational speaker".

At first glance, the motivational speaker seems to lead a glamorous and eventful life. They travel from city to city, even around the globe, to have speaking sessions. They rub elbows with celebrities, politicians, government leaders and other notable personalities. They even appear on television often, and most of them have even published books that went straight to the top of the bestseller lists.

But it is highly likely that they have gone through a lot in order to get to where they currently are.

Is education required? You might think that there is a specific bachelor's degree or course that one must finish in order to become a motivational speaker. There isn't. In fact, some of the most successful motivational speakers haven't even finished college, and yet they are established as authorities in their chosen fields, and are even being paid handsomely for it.

Are they licensed? There is no license required to become a motivational speaker, either. However, there are several agencies and organizations, such as the National Speakers Association, that issue certifications to motivational speakers. These add to the credentials of the speakers.

Are they formally trained? Perhaps "formal training" is much too strict of a phrase but, yes, there are trainings that are often undergone by aspiring speakers before they become good motivational speakers.

Now let us take a look at some of the most successful motivational speakers today.

Erick Thomas of etinspires.com – He is one example that you do not have to be highly educated in order to be a powerful motivational speaker. Thomas dropped out of high school and, for a while, spent his life on the streets as a homeless man. He used his experiences to talk about what it takes to become successful, and he has become widely known for the intensity and passion in his speeches.

Tony Robbins of tonyrobbins.com – If you want to know about how to be successful, then you'll probably appreciate hearing Tony Robbins talk about it. This charismatic speaker approaches this topic from a psychology point of view, and it works.

Nick Vujicic of nickvujicic.com – What makes Nick a power motivational speaker is how he delivers his speeches – funny, self-deprecating, optimistic – as he stands there with no arms and legs. Born without limbs, one would be expected to live with bitterness and anger, but Nick is the complete opposite, centering his talks around never giving up and staying determined in the face of adversity.

Stephen Covey of stephencovey.com – Although Covey

passed away in 2012 at the age of 79, he remains to be one of the most successful and widely known motivational speakers. Proof of his legacy are his books, most notable of which are "The 7 Habits of Highly Effective People", "The 7 Habits of Highly Effective Families", and "The Leader in Me". He is undoubtedly one of the most educated speakers, and his learnings contributed to his speeches on improving oneself to become successful.

DEFINITION OF MOTIVATIONAL SPEAKERS

Motivational Speakers can be either Platform Speakers or Keynote Speakers. Tony Robbins, for example, is definitely a Motivational Speaker but he is also clearly a Platform Speaker. He's selling stuff. He has CDs, DVDs and lots of expensive programs. T. Harv Eker is the same, but Motivational Speakers can also be Keynote Speakers. There are tons of speakers that offer motivational programs to companies and associations. Sales trainers and team-building experts come to mind, as do some leadership speakers.

It's important to understand that any Keynote Speaker, regardless of his or her category, needs to have a motivational angle to his or her speech. If it's not motivational, you won't get any referrals. Actually, there are two elements you need: motivation and humor. People learn when they laugh. And if you're funny – like, comedian funny – your referral business will explode. Seriously. Get some good laugh lines and watch your business grow. There's a direct correlation between humor and referrals!

A motivational speaker, also known as an inspirational speaker, is someone who delivers speeches with the intention of motivating or inspiring the people in the audience. Typically, he or she has a reputation as an expert on the subject being discussed, and will encourage the audience to look at things from a different perspective and to become more attentive to their own talents and abilities.

DEFINITION OF PLATFORM SPEAKERS

Platform Speakers follow a predictable pattern. Their pitch begins from the very first word. They immediately identify the problem and allude to the fact that an easy solution exists. They also reassure their audiences regularly that successful people invest in their own personal development. "If you want to be successful, you need to spend some money," they claim. The second half of their presentation is "the offer" and consists of repeated examples of the true value of the problem's solution. At the end, the price is finally revealed, usually much lower than the established value, but is immediately outdone by additional discounts if you "buy today."

Platform Speaking

About 90% of speakers are Platform Speakers. Why? Because there's no barrier to entry. Anyone can start speaking at free events and try to sell their wears. But because of that (no barrier to entry), the quality tends to be low. There's a lot of riff-raff in the free circuit, but you can indeed make a living doing it, and a lot of people do. Of course, a few make it to the big leagues – people like Tony Robbins or T. Harv Eker – but it's still Platform Speaking.

Making money as a Platform Speaker can be a struggle. You're always trying to grow your email list and create new products or programs to sell. But having said that, the high end (Tony Robbins, etc.) offers an income potential much higher than Keynote Speaking. These days, a lot of Platform Speakers actually have much broader businesses, selling information products online among other things. People like Brendon Burchard and James Malinchak come to mind. And again, those established names make a fortune. Unfortunately, most Platform Speakers never get that far.

DEFINITION OF KEYNOTE SPEAKERS

Keynote Speaking is different. As a Keynote Speaker, you're hired by an organization to speak at an event, and the only thing you're selling is your message. In fact, if you tried to sell something else (like a 3-day seminar or an expensive coaching program), you would never be hired back! As a keynote speaker, you get a check to speak. That's your payment and it would be completely inappropriate to try to make even more money by selling stuff to the audience. So the Cheap Circuit and the Pro Circuit are both Keynote Speaking circuits. You get paid, so no selling allowed.

Keynote Speaking

As a Keynote Speaker, you're always being hired by new organizations. Yes, there are some that will bring you back a second or even a third time, but the referral process usually brings you a steady stream of new clients. In fact, if you do a good job, every speaking engagement should lead to 3 or 4 more … and there are literally hundreds of thousands of organizations who host events and hire professional speakers. That means that once you get established, and if you're good, the marketing process should take care of itself.

I live in the San Francisco Bay Area and on any given week day, there are probably at least 100 speakers being paid to speak at various events around the city. There's literally tons of business. It's endless. Every single medium or large-sized business has an annual meeting, and so does every single association. And once you do a good job within a given industry sector, the referrals will lead to more opportunities for similar organizations.

Getting back to income potential, the top names in the Platform Speaking business make millions of dollars each year. I think Tony Robbins made over 15 million dollars one year. Keynote Speakers can't touch that. The upper income limit for most Keynote Speakers is about $400,000 or $500,000 per year. I break this down in more detail near the bottom of this post.

Keynote Speakers generally fall into one of four categories: motivation, inspiration, overcoming adversity and leadership. Leadership and overcoming adversity speak for themselves, but the difference between motivation and inspiration is a bit more subtle. My definitions is that motivation is the act of convincing people to do things that they already know they should be doing. By contrast, inspiration is the act of convincing people to do things that they never thought of doing until they heard your speech.

WHO IS A MOTIVATIONAL SPEAKER?

A motivational speaker is a person who gives speeches that encourage or inspire the audience. Motivational speakers (sometimes called "inspirational speakers") often tell a compelling personal life story about achieving success in the face of adversity. They may also be an author or thought-leader with expertise in personal development.

Although the term "motivational speaker" might refer to a person who shares their story on an unpaid, volunteer basis with local groups or religious organizations, skilled motivational speakers can give speeches as their primary livelihood. There are several thousand of these "professional speakers" who travel around the world, receiving speaking fees to give presentations at conferences, conventions, schools, and other events. Celebrity motivational speakers (like, say, Simon Sinek) may receive six-figure fees per appearance and give one-hundred or more speeches per year.

What Exactly Is a Motivational Speaker?

First and foremost, becoming a motivational speaker is not everyone's cup of tea. Normally, people who opt for this career choice have tons of experiences that they share with others in order to inspire and uplift them.

It's a fact that success stories are often key to making a person become better in their daily life no matter how messed up their lives may be at the moment.

Typically, the experiences that motivational speakers convey are not your run of the mill anecdotes. No, they look at life as an intriguing and profound learning experience and always deliver substantive advice. And where do they do this? Almost always, they share their wisdom in public places, such as academic events, government events, etc, in order to motivate, inspire and inform their listeners en masse.

In addition to having a ton of experiences to share, motivational speakers are also expert communicators which is crucial for this line of work. So, it goes without saying that a motivational speaker will find it incredibly difficult to stand in front of thousands of people of all ages and share their story confidently if they lack communication skills. Due to this very reason, there are hundreds of people who never share their stories.

In short, motivational speakers deliver profound and extremely useful insights that help people improve the lives of other people. They share their life-changing or uplifting messages in public, and they are consummate communicators.

So what do you think? Is the business of motivation for you? Before you answer, first check out this next section. Knowing how much motivational speakers make, may just get you off the fence and into an auditorium.

WHAT DOES A MOTIVATIONAL SPEAKER DO?

A motivational speaker, also known as an inspirational speaker, is someone who delivers speeches with the intention of motivating or inspiring the people in the audience.

The ultimate goal of a motivational speaker is to change people profoundly on an emotional and/or mental level, and to help them make some kind of professional or personal change in their lives and within themselves. People naturally tend to focus on all their problems, and the motivational speaker will help an audience to focus on the many opportunities instead, by using any number of persuasive speech tactics to inspire and motivate.

Some speakers may be hired to speak as special guests, and others travel a planned circuit of speaking engagements. The more popular motivational speakers may also write and sell inspirational books, dvd's and appear on television.

Almost all motivational speakers relate their own personal experience to an audience, which means they can come from any kind of background and use that information to inspire others. Not everyone evaluates their significant life experiences to determine if those experiences could be helpful to others. A motivational speaker is constantly reflecting on their own life to see what information would be helpful to their audiences or clients. They speak in a variety of venues like schools, company boardrooms, community centres, and conferences.

TYPES OF MOTIVATIONAL SPEAKERS

Motivational speakers relate their own experience and expertise to an audience at professional speaking gigs. Motivational speakers work in a variety of different venues, from schools to community centers, large community venues and executive boardrooms. Their purpose is to motivate others toward various goals, whether they be self-improvement, business team objectives or community initiatives. There are many different types of motivational speakers, with different areas of expertise.

Personal Development

The first type of motivational speaker is one who is meant to inspire listeners and help them find guidance and purpose in their lives. These speakers might give talks on a specific topic such as how to balance family and work or spiritual development. In some cases, they might tell personal stories of adversity and triumph to give hope to the audience. These types of motivational speakers allow individual audience members to take their own lessons from the talk and apply it to their lives in any way they see fit. Many times there is not a fixed message. Instead, these talks are meant to inspire people to take their own actions and find new perspectives.

Business

Motivational speakers can also provide guidance and encouragement to business teams at any level, from frontline salespeople to executive directors and entire staffs. Business speakers usually have expertise and experience in the field of business and many of them share their means of attaining success. In this setting, the speaker provides leadership and unity, guiding members of the business team toward enthusiasm and a common purpose. Not only can they share techniques for business success, they can also provide hope to lower-level workers that hard work pays off, often through their personal experience of rising through the ranks.

Youth Mentor

Some motivational speakers specifically address young people at schools, churches, community centers and other venues. These speakers hope to guide the youths toward healthy ambitions and a successful life, and help them to take their place as the generation of the future. Topics might include reasons to take school seriously, the payoff of studying hard, the process of finding a calling in life, how to interact in a healthy manner with others or how to develop a moral code. The goal is usually to give children some positive guidance and a sense of direction during their formative years, while guiding them to avoid the pitfalls and stumbling blocks of bad decisions, bad luck or lack of motivation.

Community

Motivational speakers can also give talks about important social and community issues. In these cases, their goals are to educate the audience about the topic at hand, giving them the power to take positive action. Alternatively, the speaker might try to direct the audience toward a certain type of action. For example, a motivational speaker might give talks to get people involved in efforts to stop littering in the community. Some speakers might have a specific plan for how to accomplish this. Aside from providing education and awareness, the speaker in this situation might relay experience with campaigns to stop littering in different communities.

ARE YOU SUITED TO BE A MOTIVATIONAL SPEAKER?

Motivational speakers have distinct personalities. They tend to be artistic individuals, which means they're creative, intuitive, sensitive, articulate, and expressive. They are unstructured, original, nonconforming, and innovative. Some of them are also enterprising, meaning they're adventurous, ambitious, assertive, extroverted, energetic, enthusiastic, confident, and optimistic.

Is becoming a motivational speaker right for me?

The first step to choosing a career is to make sure you are actually willing to commit to pursuing the career. You don't want to waste your time doing something you don't want to do.

WHAT IS THE WORKPLACE OF A MOTIVATIONAL SPEAKER LIKE?

A motivational speaker tends to work irregular hours depending on their speaking engagements, travel requirements, and how much time they need to write or refine their speeches. Highly successful speakers are in demand and will be called on to present at conferences and events all over the world. This means they can have very heavy travel schedules.

The job doesn't always stop once the conference speaking engagement is over. Many successful motivational speakers also write books, produce seminars, videos or podcasts, and may also appear on television.

DEVELOP AND IMPROVE YOUR PUBLIC SPEAKING SKILLS

Even though it should go without saying, we are going to say it because it is absolutely paramount and vital. Motivational speakers must be talented public speakers. Even the most inspiring story or message will fail to resonate if it is not delivered with intention and flair. Not all people are naturally comfortable speaking in front of large crowds. But the skill can be learned and honed through education, practice, and experience.

Here are ways to improve your public speaking abilities:

Public Speaking Classes

Many community colleges offer classes in public speaking. Curricula commonly include stage presence; how to overcome fear and gain confidence; voice regulation and modulation; how to be persuasive; body language; how to handle difficult questions; and how to create the right presentation.

Public Speaking Clubs

Toastmasters International is a world leader in communication and leadership development. The organization, which has clubs in 143 countries around the world, provides excellent opportunities for its members to improve their speaking and leadership skills.

Audio and Video Recordings

Both audio and video recordings of your speeches are crucial for you to effectively evaluate your presentation and determine if you are convincing and likely to motivate others to take action. When watching and listening to these recordings, pay close attention to the flow of your thoughts, the enunciation of your words, the tone of your voice, your hand movements and gestures, and your eye contact with the audience. As the speaker, do you exude confidence? As an audience member, are you comfortable and engaged?

Learning how to write

The majority of successful motivational speakers also know how to write. It is common for speakers to compose their own presentations and to sometimes write supplementary material that may be provided to audiences to help guide them through the presentation. In addition, many established speakers are also authors. Sometimes, people do not become motivational speakers until after they have published their work and been asked to speak at events.

Promote yourself and listen to feedback

A plan to market and sell yourself is as important as the message and perspective you want to share:

• Determine your message and identify your audience; First and foremost, know who you want to speak to and what you want to say to them! Ask yourself if your message is relevant and timely. Think about the cultural and personality characteristics of your intended audience and how they should influence the ways you communicate.

• Offer free workshops and talks; In the words of renowned international speaker Brian Tracy, 'before you can be paid to speak, you have to have given 300 free talks.' These early talks are the training ground on which to practise the craft, advertise, increase audience awareness, and receive feedback.

• Connect with your audience through social media; Use social media to make yourself accessible and easy to contact. Look for opportunities to be interviewed on podcasts. Write posts for popular blogs. Create a buzz.

• Become a member of accredited speakers' circles and bureaus;There are agencies which specialize in connecting conference organizers and meeting planners with inspirational speakers. Several of these agencies handle fee negotiations, event scheduling, and other logistics, allowing speakers to focus on their presentations. Two of the most prominent of these organizations are the National Speakers Associationand the National Speakers Bureau.

• Create a blog or website;Build a platform via blogging and podcasting about relevant topics on your own website. In other words, create a home for your content.

HOW TO HONE YOUR MOTIVATIONAL ENTREPRENEURIAL SKILLS, AND CONTRIBUTE TO A DIFFERENCE

If you have decided to turn a full-fledged entrepreneur, you have lots to cheer about as you need not physically own an office space, lead a large team, and resort to doing conventional business to earn profits. In new-age entrepreneurship, profits would come to you even without you actually doing the usual profit-and-loss business.

In this regard, one way to let your entrepreneurial juices follow is Motivational Speaking. This is believed by entrepreneurial experts to be a fast-catching trend, and the predicament actually lets you be an entrepreneur and get to make a difference in the lives of others through your inspirational speaking skills. Now, with motivating others (as a continuation of your entrepreneurial traits) being the criteria, below are 6 key ways in which you could hone your entrepreneurial ability to motivate others and make a positive difference whilst earning passive income:

Trying out minor nuances:

Now, you would neither need to organize a public speaking event to show off your motivational skills, nor need to search for people in need of positivity. You could hone your motivational speaking skills by motivating the entrepreneur in you. Talk to yourself, positively motivate and get focused to test out the waters as a motivational speaker; despite obstacles. Motivate yourself with the nuances to march ahead and be the person that people could look upto when in need of moral support.

Establish passive connect:

Now, the key trait of a motivational speaker is to establish connect; however, you need not personally sit down with people in need of motivation (active connect); you could simply use the internet as a medium to propagate your motivational talks. While speaking, ensure that you arouse the feeling of positivity by sharing personal experiences, quotes from great people (entrepreneurs here), and habits that are offbeat but required to navigate troubled waters. This becomes a passive approach whilst you are addressing people without actually physically being with them.

Make stories:

We do not refer to fabricating stories here, rather penning down your personal experiences and introducing an offbeat way to solve encountered challenges. Each such offbeat mechanism would potentially turn motivational for your audience who mostly are in need of encouragement to pursue the vagaries of life. Hence, you could pen down a successful story of yourself and how you turned entrepreneur, and use the opportunity to motivate others to do the same.

Look Within:

Get your audience to look within themselves for motivation. For this, present experiences where you have had to defy norms (personal connect) to succeed. Encourage offbeat approaches to problems. A chunk of your audience would potentially come back to you, with experiences of how they were successful by considering the self as the greatest motivational speaker. Your job would be to arouse this spirit.

Connect the dots:

Enshrine the connecting the dots approach, both for your audiences as well as yourself; here, you could educate people on how every incident that takes place would not be an eventuality but would eventually lead to potential positivity. And illustration here is the way in which a thousand squares make up a great image; people realizing this are called artists. Hence, your audience could be turned into artists (of life) as well.

Learn from your own self:

We can only speak if we are experienced and experience is nothing but what we have gone through mindfully. A person who does not experience the world mindfully will only have shallow memories and that is not the feature of a person close to enlightenment. So with your own experience you can help people. If you lack experience you are only babbling, it can never be an enlightened experience for the listener or the speaker.

WHAT MAKES A GOOD MOTIVATIONAL SPEAKER?

Can you remember an event you attended where you were completely blown away by the presenter or guest speaker? Perhaps it was a commencement address for college graduation or a conference where a passionate professional spoke of their trials and tribulations. Do you recall the passion in their voices? The excitement in their gestures? Good motivational speakers have the unique ability to inspire an entire room. Motivational keynote speakers can truly deliver thought-provoking and emotional speeches that give listeners the strength they need to reach their goals once walk out the doors. While it's essential to have a knack for public speaking, it takes more than eloquent speech to make a motivational speaker successful. It takes much effort and practice to refine the methods of motivational speaking. So, how do they do it? How do motivational speakers lift us up and inspire us to do more?

Important Qualities of Motivational Speakers

A good and well practiced motivational speaker not

only can paint a picture with their storytelling but teach a lesson and motivate individuals in a way that can relate to certain aspects of the audience's life. Most importantly, a seasoned motivational speaker can read the room and speak to the audience's needs rather than their own. Let's dive into a few more important qualities that make up a successful motivational speaker.

Passion: In order to be a successful motivational speaker for events, it's essential that one has a passion for what they do and what they speak about. Having a passion for what they do will only help them thrive as a motivational speaker. Most importantly, a motivational speaker who exudes passion in their work is someone who inspires others. An audience can pick up on a speaker's passion for what they are doing and, in turn, have more respect for them and their work.

Dynamic: With time and circumstance, the needs of individuals change all the time. Any successful motivational speaker for events will know how to navigate these circumstances to ensure that their speech is always relevant to the audience. To truly impart wisdom and inspiration on your audience, motivational speakers must display dynamic qualities. To be dynamic, a motivational speaker must always remain up to date on the latest trends in their area of expertise.

Confidence: Confidence is key when it comes to motivational speaking. If you want your audience to be enthralled with what you are trying to impart on them, it's essential that you have confidence in yourself.

A Strong Speaking Voice: Most of the time, motivational

speakers will present in front of very large audiences. Therefore, it's essential to have a strong and robust voice that will carry across the room. A seasoned motivational speaker for events has a voice that boasts influence and authority–keeping their audience focused throughout the entire presentation. Not only must a motivational speaker have a strong speaking voice, but they must speak with clarity, conciseness, and with perfect annunciation.

Empathy: Having empathy for your work and your audience is another essential quality for a motivational speaker to have. Being able to empathize with others will allow speakers to expand new depths in their work and relate to their audiences on another level. Great motivational speakers will us empathy to put themselves in their audience's shoes to get a better understanding of how they feel. Empathy will give speakers the opportunity to deliver speeches that empowers everyone in the room.

Sense of Humor: Everyone likes someone with an appropriate sense of humor. Adding humor to your speeches is one of the best ways to keep your audience enthralled. Adding jokes or fun anecdotes into your speech is a wonderful way to keep your speech fun and light-hearted in certain sections.

Engagement with the Audience

Public speaking isn't all about the monologue, and you can read more here on how engaging your audience helps. An excellent motivational speaker strives to engage the audience as much as they can. Dialogue is one of the best approaches to kill the element of boredom during the presentation.

You can achieve dialogue by making fun, asking questions, painting a picture through story-telling or conducting body-relaxing activities. A well-engaged audience will avoid being on their phones or laptops when you're talking to them.

Knowledge and Expertise

If you want to be successful at motivational speaking, be knowledgeable. More specifically, choose your area of specialization. You can't be all things in one.

When you choose an area of specialization, you'll never run out of ideas when talking to your audience. As your experience increases, you'll become an expert in that area. People will seek your services based on the knowledge you've got.

An example of a niche you could specialize in is business. You may not need to have many years of experience in business, but you'd need to read widely about it. Spending time with business gurus and learning from them would also be a plus for you.

THE ROLE OF A MOTIVATIONAL SPEAKER

The role of a motivational speaker is to deliver a speech that inspires the audience to reflect upon their own life in some profound way that gets them to change their behavior or take a specific action.

The ultimate goal for motivational speeches is to spread new ideas and inspire a positive change among listeners, whether it's a change in their mindset, lifestyle and everyday actions, their organization, or a bigger change in our society.

To accomplish this important goal, motivational speakers need to have a range of skills to stick the landing in their speeches.

Event organizers hire motivational speakers because it is a great way to engage an audience and grab their attention by driving home a specific talking point through the storytelling process.

We all remember those high school games when the coach is screaming and getting the squad all hyped up and ready for the game. We're in the moment, nothing else matters. The only thing that you're thinking about are the words he's saying and how bad you want to make that game winning tackle or catch, that game winning basket, or make an unbelievable dig that sends the crowd on their feet. Then once that whistle blows...all you're thinking about is that exact moment in time, that next play, that next serve. Everything before the game is completely forgotten, especially the words your coach were screaming right before the game.

So what is the point of a motivational speaker? Of course he or she is to inspire and motivate in the short term, but inevitably, you have to CONSISTENTLY motivate yourself to get out of bed that next day and go to work. I believe his or her purpose is to be a reminder of all the work you have done or will do, the person you have become and the person you can be. It's not the 30 seconds that he/she says right before a game, it's the hundreds of 30-second clips you listen to daily and embed in your brain. We become what values and morals we live by. Our morals and values are developed over time from our thoughts and beliefs. Our thoughts and beliefs are formed by the content we consistently fill our heads with. So it would make sense if we consistently fill our heads with motivating positive thoughts, how do we not BECOME positive and motivated. Are there times when things are rough? Absolutely. Are there times when you don't want to get out of your bed because it's so comfortable and amazing? No question. But during those tough times, it's how we respond that determine the outcome. And when it all boils down to it, we'll respond in ordinance with our thoughts and beliefs.

So don't listen to a motivational speech just 20 minutes before a game or just after you experience those tough times. Get on YouTube, Listen to them everyday before you go to work, in the shower, or on your run. Just make it part of your routine. Get hyped for the opportunity you have today and the problems you can solve for tomorrow!

How long is a motivational speech?

The speech's length varies depending on the topic and the setting, but common types of motivational speeches last from 60 to 90 minutes.

This duration is long enough so that the speaker can effectively deliver all the points he or she wants to make, while not too long that it will lose the audience's interest and attention.

Depending on the topic, the speech will cover anecdotes from the speaker's experience, bigger context from our society, learning's and immediate actions that the audience can take to start problem-solving their issues.

Although this is a relatively short amount of time, the impact you see after a motivational speech often lasts much longer.

Businesses, youth organizations, non-profits, and communities witness long-term benefit from motivational speeches, thanks to their ability to instill a sense of purpose among their people.

How motivational speakers prepare

Motivational speakers spend a lot of time learning and reflecting on their personal experiences, especially those that profoundly affect their perceptions of the human experience.

Inspiring speakers often have unique approaches towards their past hardships and trauma, they view these as lessons and opportunity to grow.

Their stories are often extraordinary tales of healing and growth, that's why their ideas are impactful, they help listeners gain perspective for their own negative experiences and feel inspired to change their current situation.

Motivational speakers are experts

Many motivational speakers have years of experience and professional training before they start their careers in speaking.

Whether it's entrepreneurship, psychology and counseling, research, learning's from their personal journey, or other areas, their expertise is what makes motivational speakers seem compelling.

They have the ability to translate academic concepts and theories into simple, easy-to-understand ideas to help readers investigate their own experiences and view them from objective eyes.

This gives the listeners the clarity and perspective needed to tackle their own challenges.

Motivational speakers tell great stories

If you have ever attended a long, boring lecture in school, you know that great story-telling abilities are among the most important skills to get any ideas heard.

Not only are the best motivational speakers equipped with personal experience and technical expertise, but their delivery needs to make a lasting impression among the audience.

Therefore, the stories they craft for their live events need to be interesting, inspiring and memorable to instill change in the mindsets of their listeners.

Just like fables and pearls of wisdom, these stories offer learning's that the audience can reflect upon and implement in their everyday lives.

Motivational speakers have charisma
Great speakers have a natural gravitas that can captivate a crowd and make you want to believe them.

Each word they speak, each pause they take, every action and body language is well-rehearsed to help the message reach listeners and resonate with them.

This takes years of practice speaking in front of an audience, but the results are apparent – you remember their messages, you believe them and feel compelled to take actions.

When they are on stage, they are representing you and your organization which means that they must be likeable and relatable.

Motivational speakers inspire change
One of the goals of a speaker is to guide people towards

taking some form of action in their life or business.

Not only do they inspire a change in attitude, but they also lead to immediate actions.

Motivational speeches guide listeners through a series of simple steps, sometimes, only daily, small changes that have a lasting impact in the long run.

That's what makes them more impactful than the average TED talk – the crowd leaving a motivational speech often radiates a bigger sense of purpose and feels more motivated to change.

For this reason, companies and organizations can benefit greatly from a motivational speech, which can fuel their employees with an intense desire to change for the better and guide the organization towards a sustainable culture and purposeful business practice.

Motivational speakers are creators

In addition to traveling to their speaking arrangements, motivational speakers also create other content to spread their messages to a wider audience.

They write self-help books, biographies, make You-Tube videos, write blogs, host podcasts and appear on television.

These contents never steer too far from the speaker's expertise, they act as self-learning devices to help listeners retain the message longer and employ the techniques shared more effectively.

STEPS TO BECOME A PROFESSIONAL MOTIVATIONAL SPEAKER

Becoming a motivational speaker appeals to many people who have a passion for telling their stories of success. Motivational speakers come from many different backgrounds and industries. Inspired by experiences from their personal or work lives, motivational speakers may turn a unique anecdote or idea into a full-time career.

Developing your public speaking strategy may come naturally or take some work. Experiment with different ways to deliver your message and continue to network with other professionals to build your credibility. Follow this series of steps to start your own inspirational journey:

Start with a subject you know well and Develop unique content to talk on

You must have a passion for the subject you wish to promote. If it's not important to you, you'll have a hard time convincing other people that it should matter to them. If you're not sure where to start, write down a list of subjects you feel strongly about and that you'd like to share with others. If you possess expert-level knowledge in the subject, it adds to your content and credibility. Chances are, you already know what you want to speak about.

Guide to Choosing a Speech Topic

Choosing a speech topic can sometimes feel harder than giving the actual speech. I have provided a simple framework for filtering down the number of possible topics to speak about.

When deciding on a speech or presentation topic, you might naturally want to talk about something you know very well. Although this is important, it's only part of the equation when deciding on a suitable speech topic.

You need to ask yourself three questions about the topic, linking your expertise, passion and the audience.

Three questions to ask yourself

When deciding on a speech topic, ask yourself these three questions:

How much do I know about the topic? Your audience needs to recognise you as a credible speaker and being knowledgeable about your topic is an easy way to do this. A good understanding will help you explain difficult parts of the topic and give you more confidence during the questions and answers session.

Am I passionate about the topic? Your passion on the

topic will affect all areas of your delivery, including body language, eye contact and energy levels. If you are interested in the topic, you'll engage with the audience better and generally make for a more interesting speech.

Will the audience be interested in the topic? If the audience doesn't see how they can learn something useful from your topic, they'll either not turn up or switch off early during the speech. Remember that your speech topic needs to contain value for the audience.

Write down a list of possible speech topics in line with the type of speech or presentation you are giving – is it a TED talk? A commencement speech? A conference presentation? A talk at your local club? Once you have this list, go through each of the three questions and put them into the segments

What type of audience will you be speaking to?

In order to talk about a topic your audience care about, you'll need to perform a quick analysis of your audience. There are several methods to do this, including:

Find out if there are any other speakers and their topics if possible (if they are very technical, it give you an idea of the type of audience)

Look at the event social media and read through previous comments

Contact the event host to ask for more information about the types of audience that usually attend (for example, how many are international)

Find out the size of the audience (this may determine the structure of your speech, including where to do the question and answer session, whether to include humour etc.)

There are a few audience characteristics which might determine the speech topic you select, including:

• Average age

• Gender (will it be a mostly female audience?)

• Ethnic background

• Types of career (is it a business focussed event?)

• Knowledge of the topic

Segment 1: Great speech topics

Topic segment: You are knowledgeable and passionate about the topic, and the audience is interested in it as well.

This is the perfect combination, and a good speaker draws speech topics from this segment all the time. Your knowledge of the topic assures that you'll be confident. You enjoy talking about the topic so you'll be passionate about it. On top of that, you have an enthusiastic, open audience.

When you end up speaking about topics in this segment, you'll have a high chance of delivering a memorable and engaging speech.

Segment 2: Good content but lacking enthusiasm

Topic segment: You know the topic well and your audience finds it interesting, however you lack enthusiasm for the topic.

Speeches in this segment will lack enthusiasm and might be delivered in a monotone voice with poor body language.

An example of a topic in this segment

When you finish a large body of research, for example towards the end of a PhD, you'll usually have to present the results to an audience. The audience are usually invested in your topic and interested to hear about what you have to say. You also know plenty about the topic as you've spent years researching it.

How to make this a segment 1 topic

Ask yourself what motivated you to learn about the topic in the first place. Try and find that enthusiasm again.

You can try asking your potential audience what gets them excited about the topic. This might spark some interested in the topic again for you as you'll understand the benefit you are giving the audience. You can also guide your presentation around the audience answers and you now know what they are excited by.

Segment 3: Great speech topics for a different audience

Topic segment: You know and find the speech topic interesting, however your audience does not.

An example of a topic in this segment

Perhaps you are the creator of an open source project for a new programming language. You may well love what you are developing and know everything about it. However if you are speaking at a local conference, the audience may not be as enthusiastic.

How to make this a segment 1 topic

You've analysed your audience and find that the audience doesn't care much for this topic. You need to understand how you can link the topic to something your audience will find interesting, through story-telling, metaphors, diagrams and any other suitable method.

If you use body language and eye contact well, you might be able to engage the audience even if the topic isn't of too much interest to them.

Tip

A topic in this segment is best saved for a different audience. If you find the right event and audience, this would a great topic to talk about and you'll be both passionate and informed about the topic.

Segment 4: Interesting topics you know nothing about

Topic segment: This is a topic both you and your audience find interesting, however your knowledge for the topic is lacking.

You may not know enough about the topic for you to appear credible in the eyes of the audience. Your lack of knowledge on the topic may get revealed in the questions and answers session after the speech.

An example of a topic in this segment

Imagine you've recently taken up a new hobby, impressionism painting, for example, and want to talk about tips for impressionist artists at a local gallery. You may love the topic and so will your audience, however as you're new to the hobby, you won't have any expertise in it.

How to make this a segment 1 topic

This is one of the best segments to be in and there are a few approaches you can take to bring yourself into the middle segment:

Build up your knowledge of the topic over time. If you have a big event such as a TED Talk coming up and a few weeks before you're speaking, a topic in this segment could work well. Your passion and an engaged audience provide excellent motivation for your speech to succeed.

If you're speaking to a smaller group, you can try to facilitate a discussion between yourself and the audience members. You might start by giving a short speech which opens up some conversation points and then letting the audience discuss new ideas and solutions.

Segment 5: Speech topics someone else should deliver

Topic segment: Your audience care a lot about this topic, however you neither know or care about it.

How to make this a segment 1 topic

This is a tough topic to bring into segment 1. You need to be passionate about the topic in order to learn about it. Sometimes when you start learning a topic, you'll find yourself becoming more passionate the better you understand it. However this takes time and you're better leaving this topic for someone else to deliver.

Tip

Don't try to wing this topic. You'll be shown up in the questions and answers session, as well as lack enthusiasm while delivering the speech. Your credibility will be ruined.

Segment 6: Topics you know but don't interest you

Topic segment: You know this topic well but neither you nor your audience find it interesting.

How to make this a segment 1 topic

You can try to find your passion for the topic and link it to your audience's interests. This is going to be difficult and you'll be better off finding another topic.

Segment 7: Personal hobbies, not speech topics

Topic segment: A speech topic you find interesting but don't know much about and your audience doesn't find it too interesting.

How to make this a segment 1 topic

Of the three outer segments, this is the easiest to convert to a great speech topic. Having passion for a topic provides great motivation, and can motivate you to develop your own expertise, as well as seek out reasons why the audience should care.

Segment 8: Topics neither you nor your audience care about

Topic segment: Disaster zone – you don't know about the topic or care much about it, and neither does your audience.

How to make this a segment 1 topic

This would be very difficult. It's best to choose another topic and not to waste your time on topics in this segment.

An example of a topic in this segment

Talks that fall into this dead segment are quite common. After taking a train the trainer course, you might be asked to coach other employees at your company which is mandatory for them to attend. You don't know the topic very well, and it doesn't excite you. Your audience's attendance is mandatory, but they don't really want to be there either.

Understand your target audience

As much as you'd like to have everyone love your message, not everyone will. Know that this is okay and expected. Focus on connecting with your most engaged audience members and create content designed to resonate with them. You'll learn a lot about your followers through engagement on social media, message boards, and other forms of correspondence like email and fan mail.

Giving a speech in front of an audience can be nerve-wracking. All eyes are on you, and your audience is expecting to hear something engaging and interesting from your speech. Whether you are an experienced orator or a public-speaking novice, it's important to research your audience before you give your speech. By catering to your audience, you can ensure your speech is successful and meets the goals you're looking to achieve.

Understand the Benefits of Audience Analysis

The role of the audience in communication is highly important. After all, if your audience isn't interested in what you're saying or doesn't understand the terminology you use, then your speech may fall flat. In order to ensure your audience pays attention, it's critical to research to whom you're speaking and understand their preferences and motivations.

Audience analysis can help you to:

- Meet the specific needs of your audience group
- Give a memorable and impactful speech
- Achieve your business objectives
- Create lasting and meaningful relationships with audience members
- Build a business network or helpful peers

When you take the time to research to whom you're speaking, you are able to write a speech that is tailored to what your audience needs to know and to topics about which they care. This enables you to get your message across more accurately. For example, a speech to your employees will be written differently than a speech to customers. It's important to review background and context before writing your speech.

Plan in Advance

Conduct your audience research early so you have plenty of time to prepare your speech based on their interests. Ask the host of the event for details on who will be attending. You can also send out a short survey to people who will be attending to gather critical data. Using published market research can also help you to understand those to whom you will be speaking.

Review Their Demographics

Start your audience analysis by understanding the demographics of the group to whom you're speaking. This includes:

- Age range

- Gender
- Ethnicity
- Religion
- Sexual orientation
- Education
- Job
- Salary
- Social status

These characteristics can greatly affect the way people understand and react to your message. For example, if you're giving a speech to your senior employees who are in executive-level positions with good salaries, their interests will differ from your junior-level employees who are in entry-level positions and may be paying off hefty student loans.

Keep in mind that demographics are not the only factor your should consider. For example, if the majority of your audience members are age 16 to 20, you may assume that they are interested in social media and music. This doesn't mean that your entire speech needs to be focused around those things. Knowing your audience demographics can help you frame your speech, but you should keep in mind that your audience may be interested in other things as well.

Delve Into Their Behavior
Understanding your audience's demographic characteristics can help you to discern their behavioral qualities. This includes:

Priorities: What do they hold important above all else? What are they more likely to purchase?

Goals: What do they hope to achieve in the short term and long term?

Concerns: What kinds of challenges do they face in their day-to-day lives with which you can help?

Fears: What keeps them up at night? About what do they worry?

By delving into your audience's behavior, you can make educated guesses about what they value and the things about which they care. For example, if your audience is concerned about the environment and is interested in the factors that affect climate change, they may want to know more about your company's efforts to use sustainable materials in your manufacturing process.

Tailoring your speech based on your audience's interests can help you create content that resonates deeply with your audience, making your speech more impactful. If you're talking to a group of prospects who prioritize health and fitness, for example, take care to discuss how your product can make their workouts easier.

Create an Audience Persona
Once you have gathered your audience analysis research, create an audience persona. This is a character who is representative of the majority of your audience. Include their demographic and behavioral qualities and make educated guesses about any information you may be missing.

For example, if you know that they are young parents, you can assume that they may be interested in financial planning for their future or looking for low-budget entertainment options they can do with little kids.

Having all of this information summarized succinctly in one place makes it easy to understand at a glance. Keep your audience persona handy when you are working on your speech so you can reference it when you need more details about the things in which your audience is interested. The audience persona can also be a valuable resource for future speeches you make to this audience.

Establish the Objective of Your Speech
Keeping your audience analysis in mind, identify the main goal of your speech.

Inform: Telling employees about a new company policy or updating them on quarterly results.

Entertain: Engaging guests at an industry dinner.

Persuade: Convincing prospects and customers to make a purchase.

Inspire: Motivating investors to support your company.

Understanding your key objective based on your audience will help you to craft a speech that is highly targeted, ensuring you keep your audience's attention throughout.

Outline What Your Audience Knows and Doesn't Know
When working on your speech, it's critical to know your audience's level of experience with the topic on which you're focusing. Ask yourself:

How much does your audience already know, and what

information are they missing?

Are they aware of what information they don't know?

What is their level of familiarity with the subject matter?

Do they understand industry jargon?

If the audience of a speech doesn't understand the words you're using, for example, you will not be able to get your message across. On the other hand, if the audience isn't aware that they are missing any information, then you have to provide them with some context before you begin your speech. Alternatively, if they are already experts in the field about which you're talking, then covering the basics may bore them and create a loss of credibility for you.

Imagine you're presenting to a group of investors who know nothing about the kind of technology your company creates. In this speech, it would be beneficial to discuss the revolutionary qualities of your technology and even show them a short demo. However, if those investors are already familiar with your industry, then you can skip to talking about the financial benefits and show a more advanced demo.

Keep the Venue in Mind
Audience analysis in public speaking also includes reviewing the characteristics of the venue to ensure it suits your guests. Consider:

- Accessibility
- Seating

- Acoustics
- Room temperature
- Distractions

For example, if your speech is for elderly people who may have mobility issues, a large arena with many stairs will not be ideal for your audience. Whenever possible, adjust your venue to match the needs of your guests so they feel comfortable in the setting.

Keep in mind that the time and day of your speech also need to fit with your audience's schedules. A speech for parents of young children that is late in the evening may result in a low turnout if the parents need to get a babysitter in order to come to your event. A speech to your employees held on a weekend may be an inconvenience and may affect their work-life balance. Consider how easy it is for your guests to be there and adjust accordingly.

HOW TO FIND YOUR TARGET AUDIENCE

1. Use Google Analytics to learn more about your customers.

Google Analytics is such an expansive tool, and is great for obtaining demographic details about your audience, as well as their interests. Recall from above that this is critical information that helps locate a target audience.

With Google Analytics, you'll be able to see website insights, and it's broken into different sections, like age, gender and location. These sections are labelled clearly on the dashboard and provide colorful graphs for you to interpret.

Above is an example of the age overview in the Audiences portion of Google Analytics. Notice the breakdown of the numbers and how the graphs give you an excellent visual. This tool can be a great asset into getting a really great insight into who's visiting your website and how your content fits into their lives.

2. Create a reader persona to target blog content.

With reader personas, you'll never forget who you're writing for. The good thing about reader personas is that you should closely align them to your buyer persona;

they should be nearly identical.

This is because your blog should contain content that'll be useful for your readers. Marketers probably want to read blogs about digital media, for example. It builds the reputation of your company to consumers.

The difference between a reader persona and a buyer persona is that a reader persona generally focuses on the challenges your persona might face. How can you write content that solves those challenges with blog posts?

For example, if one of the challenges you've identified in your buyer persona is "Marketing Mario wants to find a solution to low ROI on ad spending," you can use a reader persona to think of content that surrounds helping that challenge.

3. Look at social media analytics.

When are your followers most engaged with your social media channels?

Is it when you post a funny meme on Instagram or create a poll on Twitter? By taking a look at these questions, you can get a couple of clues into what content your audience is interested in, thus, filling in one of the parts needed to find a target audience.

Every social channel is different and has a different audience, so looking at your analytics across all platforms are important. For example, Twitter tends to have a younger audience, while Facebook tends to have an older one. On the same note, Twitter is based on short-form content, while on Facebook, you can post long-form content and videos.

Instagram is a visually-based social media platform, so content that's graphically stunning would thrive on the channel. Knowing these things, you can begin to plan your strategy accordingly.

Analytics can tell you who is looking at your profile. What's more, they can tell you what's working and what's not working, content-wise.

By posting content your audience is more interested in, you can gain followers that are in your target market.

4. Use Facebook Insights.

If you have a Facebook page, this tool is golden for you. Facebook gives every Page a huge set of insights, for free. These insights work similarly to Google Analytics — you'll receive critical information needed to create a target audience.

By accessing the People tab on your Insights dashboard, you can see who and from where your visitors are. Below is an example of how Facebook shows location demographics. It seems that a primary location is the east coast, so it's safe to say that part of the target audience for this page is located in east coast cities.

Other areas Facebook focuses on include interests and integrations with other social media platforms, like Twitter. The insights report tells you the lifestyle of your audience, such as if they purchase items online.

Insights like these can help you far into your campaign planning, past finding a target audience, so it's a worthwhile tool to check on every now and then.

5. Check up on website performance.

Monitor your best- and worst-performing content areas on your website. Your website can be the introduction to your company for a lot of your target audience, so sprucing up what interests them is a great way to attract more audience members.

By looking at what blog posts or landing pages are captivating your audience, you can repurpose content that isn't and promote the content that is. For instance, if your blog post about email marketing was a hit with audiences, share it on your socials to expand your reach.

6. Engage with social media audiences.

Interacting with social media followers is so important, because they're your audience. When you create your buyer persona, they're the users you should look to. If you don't have social media accounts yet, remember to keep this step in mind.

Ask your followers what they want to see, use tools like Instagram Stories and replies to get their response for how/what you're doing. Whatever engagement you get, positive or negative, can influence how you attract more audience members.

For example, try tweeting out something that invites a CTA, like "Send us a picture of your favorite outfit to wear with our new hats!" This evokes a response, responses you can analyze the language of and imitate to grow your audience.

BUILD A SOCIAL MEDIA PRESENCE

At this point, you have your brand, and you have your website. Now, let's start bringing people to it! Increasingly over the last few years, because so many event planners and decision-makers search for speakers online, one of the most effective ways to catch their attention is through social media. In addition to posts about your message and area of expertise, maintaining a social presence also shows the world who you are. What companies have you worked with? Do you work nationally or internationally? Are you more of a strict presence on stage or a funny one? Each of these questions can be answered through social posts. However, depending on the social platform you're talking about, one strategy may be more appropriate than another.

Facebook Strategy Basics

To begin with, let's look at Facebook. Launched by tech lovers and then Harvard students Mark Zuckerberg, Dustin Moskovitz, Chris Hughes and Eduardo Saverin in 2004, Facebook exploded almost immediately. In fact, by the end of its first year, the platform had over one million users across the world, providing fast and convenient connections on a scale unheard of before. Since then, Facebook has grown to more than 44,000 employees across North America, Latin America, Europe, Middle East, Africa and Asia and more than a billion user profiles. Nevertheless, despite their size, their goals remain the same, including "Give People a Voice," "Build

Connection and Community," and "Promote Economic Opportunity".

In the context of speaking, the promotion of economic opportunity is especially important. Because of this, it's important to strategize your Facebook presence. That way, you can use your Facebook profile for connecting with friends and family and your Facebook page for connecting with potential clients. On your Facebook page, remember three things above all else: be consistent, diverse, and engaging. Consistency is important both where posting and branding are concerned. Essentially, in order to market yourself as a speaker on Facebook, you need to post regularly and keep your posts' content on-brand.

That brings me to the second tip: diversifying your content. Including images, articles, or videos in your posts is not only eye-catching. It also allows you to share more with your viewer. In the same way, remember, in each post, to engage with people. If you can tag another speaker or client, do it! If you can mention, "Comment your thoughts below" have at it. The more you can connect with your audience on social media, the more likely one of them will want to be in your audience when you're on stage, too.

Using Hashtags in Facebook Posts

Another way to attract attention to your Facebook page is through the use of hashtags. Fundamentally, hashtags are words or numbers written without spaces and preceded by the pound (#) symbol. Within the speaking industry, a few commonly used hashtags are #professionalspeaker, #speakingbusiness, and #conferencespeaker, for example. For decision-makers, tracking these hashtags means easily finding speakers for their events. This makes it crucial that you include appropriate hashtags in your Facebook posts. That way, event planners can effortlessly find your Facebook page, see how great you are, and hire you.

As a side note, Hootsuite, SproutSocial, and Buffer are three tools for scheduling social media posts ahead of time.

Twitter Strategy Basics

After Facebook, let's move on to Twitter. Like Facebook, when it was originally launched by Jack Dorsey, Noah Glass, Biz Stone, and Evan Williams in 2006, Twitter was intended to act as a platform for personal connections. Allowing for only 280 characters per post, the interface is best used for succinct messages and thoughts. This originally made it the perfect platform for sharing personal thoughts and opinions and breaking recent news. Because it's considered socially acceptable to post more than once a day on Twitter, or "tweet," rather, this trend has continued into the present.

That said, in addition to personal thoughts and news, in recent years, Twitter has been used more and more for business news as well. For better or for worse, with the election of Donald Trump to the US Presidency in

2016, the world saw Twitter used for the first time as a way to communicate to the masses, share personal and professional ideas, and influence public opinion.

In your speaking business, the same principles and opportunities apply. Although on a smaller scale, using Twitter effectively to market yourself as a speaker allows you to reach a broad audience and share your message with them. Just as with Facebook, using Twitter means setting up a unique profile for your speaking business, keeping it consistent with your brand, and posting regularly. On the flip side, unlike Facebook, you can tweet more than once daily, making it especially useful if you're promoting an event while on site.

Using Hashtags in Twitter Posts

Twitter is also similar to Facebook in its use of hashtags in each post. Arguably, Twitter was the first major social media platform to use hashtags. Because of this, it's important that not only your tweets as a whole are tailored to your message, consistent, and on-brand. Your hashtags also need to meet these criteria. It's also important, as with the use of hashtags on any social profile, to test out those that work best for your speaking business. Remember, while hashtags like #professionalspeaker and #keynotespeaker are fine, they're also used all the time. Throw in a few unique ones to add some of your own style or try using them contextually, rather than including them all at the end in a string. Depending on your followers, one approach may be better than another, and you may just not know it yet.

Tip: While Donald Trump's use of Twitter is notable in many ways, remember that you don't need to capitalize full words, as from a purely grammatical standpoint, that looks bad. Remember also to keep things brief. If your message is too long for a single tweet, condense it so that it fits the character limit. This makes your message more likely to be read and more memorable for the reader.

Instagram Strategy Basics

Of the social platforms we've discussed, although each is changing constantly, one more than any other is still growing in popularity. I'm talking about the almighty Instagram. Founded in 2010 by Kevin Systrom and Mike Krieger, Instagram is the newest of the four main social platforms I'll break down in this guide. Like Facebook and Twitter, Instagram was created for personal use, originally, and has since blossomed into a massive network for businesses as well. Because of this, many of the strategies used to market yourself as a speaker on Facebook and Twitter also apply here. These include, once again, creating an account specific to your speaking business rather than your personal affairs, posting regularly, and tailoring every post, image, and video to your personal brand.

However, unlike Facebook, Twitter, and LinkedIn, Instagram requires that every post include an image or video. Because of this, your Instagram posts don't just need engaging captions. They also need engaging and diverse content. In fact, because of Instagram's requirements for visual components, when building your account, think of your profile page like a canvas. When someone visits your profile page, they should be able to see your brand colors and general style as they scroll through your feed. Are you more modern when it comes to your personal style, or more traditional? Are you a "bright colors" kind of person or more "subtle and dark"? Through the design of your Instagram posts, you can not only answer these questions and show a bit of your personality. You can also catch people's attention, so they want to dive deeper into your profile. Win win!

Using Hashtags in Instagram Posts

Additionally, just as with Facebook and Twitter, you can also attract attention on Instagram through the use of hashtags. Hashtags on Instagram can be used to (a) reach a wider audience than would normally see your account and (b) consistently show up within a given niche or industry. For example, if you search for "#speaking-business" on Instagram, you'll find a ton of posts from Jane Atkinson. As the owner of Speaker Launcher and the Wealthy Speaker School, Jane uses this hashtag to get in front of people looking for speaking business information. From there, through the content of their posts, they say, "Hey, we can help!" In the context of event planners, you can do the same thing!

All of that said, when using hashtags, there are a few things to remember. First, rather than using 2-3 hashtags contextually like on Twitter, on Instagram, you can include up to 30 hashtags per post. Ideally, you should add a comment below your post with your hashtags all together in a paragraph. That way, they don't distract from your caption but you can still "rank" for them. After that, just remember to test continuously. The more you can try out new hashtags, the more likely you are to get in front of the right people.

LinkedIn Strategy Basics

Last but not least, let's not forget LinkedIn! Unlike Facebook, Twitter, and Instagram, LinkedIn is and has always been, first and foremost, a professional community rather than a personal one. Since it was launched in 2003 by Reid Hoffman, LinkedIn has grown to more than 660 million users worldwide. Because of this, their mission to "connect the world's professionals to make them more productive and successful" has exploded, creating a vast web of connections across the globe. As you begin to use LinkedIn to market yourself as a speaker, the same extensive network available to all of those users also opens to you. This makes it easier than ever to get your name and profile in front of event planners, nationally or internationally.

To begin, using LinkedIn as a marketing platform requires a company page (separate from your personal LinkedIn profile), consistent branding and posting, and diverse content. However, because of LinkedIn's professional focus, highlighting your credentials is especially important. Unlike your profiles on the other social platforms I've covered, your LinkedIn profile has specific sections for outlining your work experience, awards, and certifications, both as a speaker and an expert in your focus industry. Additionally, just like people can leave reviews on your company Facebook page, people can review you, as a professional, on your LinkedIn profile page.

Combined, your accolades and the recommendations of others make your profile a powerful tool in selling to event planners. When posting on LinkedIn, you can also add to your credibility independently by sharing or writing articles geared towards your target audience. In short, the more others are raving about you and the more you can show your skills, the more confident event planners who look at your profile will be (i.e. the more likely they'll hire you).

Using Hashtags in LinkedIn Posts

Finally, as with the other social channels we walked through, you can also use hashtags on LinkedIn. Unsurprisingly, the same benefits of using hashtags elsewhere also apply on LinkedIn, including appearing in front of decision-makers or connecting with past audience members. However, just like posting on LinkedIn, it's important that your hashtags have a professional focus rather than a personal one. So, for example, while the hashtags "#CareerEndingTwitterTypos" or "#WhyIQuit" might be funny in a Twitter post, they're not appropriate for LinkedIn.

It's also recommended that, rather than using hashtags contextually, as seen on Twitter, hashtags on LinkedIn and Facebook can also be included at the end of the post. This is partly due to the greater number of characters allowed on LinkedIn and Facebook. However, it also allows you to more easily add hashtags without distracting from your caption. It's kind of like hashtags on Instagram, where you can add them all outside of your caption (although hashtags on LinkedIn aren't nearly as important as on Instagram, when it comes to marketing).

CREATING & MAINTAINING A SPEAKER WEBSITE

First and foremost, let's talk about websites. As far as marketing is concerned, if you don't already have a website, this is your top priority. Without a website, not only are you unable to attract potential clients through other marketing channels, such as paid advertising. You're also unable to showcase your credentials and speaking experience without having a conversation. As a speaker, the latter is especially important because of your busy schedule. After all, if you're bouncing from event to event and trying to make sales in between, you don't have a lot of time to spare. A website allows event planners to find you and get a sense of whether they want to hire you within a quick glance. Because of this, to market yourself as a speaker, a website is key.

On the flip side, if you already have a website, refreshing or rebranding it can be equally useful. Besides updating your list of past clients, redesigning your website allows you to put a new face on your speaking business. Still using stock photos from the early 2000s? Is your website mobile friendly and designed to adapt to different devices? These are just two reasons, among many, to give your website a facelift and get it up to speed with today's design trends.

Designing Your Personal Brand

That said, before rebranding your website, it's important to focus internally. Because speaking businesses are highly personal, rebranding or creating your brand has to represent you. This means that in working to market yourself as a speaker, you have to first define how you want people to see you as a person.

Ultimately, your personal brand should encapsulate your traits, values, and audience. Identifying your traits is arguably the easiest of these and involves your appearance as well as your actions. For example, looking at George Clooney, we see by his body language and tone that he is self-assured but approachable. In his attire, we see his class. In the same way, look at your own brand and comportment and ask yourself, "What words do I want people to use when describing me and my speaking business?" These words tie in closely to your values, the key issues and topics that are important to you and your stance on each one.

Finally, the last step of your personal brand is identifying your audience. When you begin to market yourself as a speaker, the more efficient path to prosperity is specificity. Look at your character traits and your personal values and ask, "Who can benefit from my knowledge the most?" In some cases, there can be a variety of industries waiting to benefit from your work. However, it's important to narrow your focus to a few select groups, so you can tailor your marketing efforts to them later on. One of the most common phrases our chief marketing officer, Taylorr, throws around is "niches lead to riches" and he's right! The more specific your focus, the more efficiently you can explain your value to the people in question and the more easily you can sell your services.

Recommended Branding & Design Services

Once you've outlined your personal brand, it's time to launch into design. Depending on your comfort level, there are a few options for creating or redesigning your website. The first option is hiring a design firm to do the work for you. Although this can be expensive, working with professional web designers comes with many benefits. For one thing, they know the technical side of building or changing websites better than many speakers do. There are, of course, exceptions to this rule, but for many speakers, the back end of their website can be difficult to navigate. Additionally, besides the technological hurdles, web designers are also helpful in their design skills. Again, there are many exceptional speakers to this rule, but in the average speaking business, the owner doesn't have the knowledge of current design trends to tackle their website with ease. Plus, they don't have the time!

DIY Branding & Design Tools

Before we get into choosing a team to do it for you, what if you want to do it yourself? . As a result, I've not only come across the marketing techniques I'll cover later in this guide. I've also found some incredible DIY design tools.

Of these tools, by far, the one that I use the most is Canva. Launched in 2012 in Sydney, Australia, Canva's mission is "to allow you to design anything and publish anywhere". Available on desktop and mobile devices, it's definitely one of the most accessible design options for speakers. Additionally, with an intuitive interface and thousands of templates, it makes it easy to peek into the world of graphic design. That way, even with a small budget, you can take control of your brand. You can also handle a large variety of branding projects, including business cards, flyers, and social posts. Basically, if you can think of a project, Canva likely has a template for it. Plus, it starts for free!

Combine Canva with photos, and you can bring designs together in minutes. Although photography from your own events is preferable, through sites like Unsplash and Pexels, not only can you find high-quality photos (in other words, not the cringe-worthy images of smiling models from the 1990s). You can also find high-resolution images available for free. In the context of design, these are especially important if you want to use them on your website or a large printed project.

For more design tools, check out a few of my other favorites below:

- PowerPoint and Keynote (slide show design for Windows and Mac, respectively)
- The Noun Project (icons)
- InVision Studio (digital design)
- Prezi (interactive presentation software)

Choosing a Domain Host

After outlining your brand, it's time to start the website construction process. The first step in this process is choosing a host for your domain. If you are new to buying and hosting domains, your domain is the string of words, letters, or numbers that you enter in the URL to identify your website. Basically, your domain is the ID for your website, so others online can find it. Your domain registrar is where you buy your domain name, and your domain host is the platform that houses your website's records and the live version of your website. In some cases, your domain registrar and domain host are managed by the same company. Within the speaking industry, a few common examples of this are Wix and Squarespace. These companies and others that combine domain registration and hosting aim to simplify the process of creating and maintaining your website.

Besides Wix and Squarespace, there are several additional options for combination domain registration and hosting. Among speakers, two of the most commonly used are GoDaddy and BlueHost. Both of these platforms are known for their general ease of use and affordability when it comes to purchasing a domain. Additionally, they also provide 24/7 support, so if you get stuck, you have someone at hand right away. However, what they have in support, they lack in long-term features. For both GoDaddy and BlueHost websites, while they're easy to build, they generally lack the robust plugins and features available through more expensive building platforms, such as WordPress. This makes them more difficult to extensively customize and scale with your speaking business. From a security standpoint, GoDaddy also surcharges a minimum of $64 per year for your SSL certificate, giving you less bang for your buck in the long run.

Choosing a Website Builder

Now that you have your brand and your domain, all that's left to do is make it a reality by creating your website. As mentioned in the last section, my favorite, when it comes to web design platforms, in WordPress. Although we've worked on several other platforms, both myself and our lead website guru, Taylorr, come back to WordPress time and time again for a number of reasons. To begin with, at only $8 per month, it's an easy-to-navigate and affordable way to design your site your way. It's also set up from the beginning with tons of themes and plugins, so you can add personality to your website without having to learn to code. For the majority of speaking businesses, this is a huge win, especially since you should ideally know how to manage your site without a developer on hand.

Another reason we gravitate towards WordPress is their companion tools, including Elementor. Created specifically for WordPress, Elementor is essentially a drag-and-drop software for building and customizing web pages. Like WordPress, besides including pre-built themes for you to start with, it also comes with a variety of widgets. These features allow you to add custom fields, animations, and layouts to a page in a single click. They also make it easy for you or another member of your team to edit or update your site, even with very little knowledge of how websites are constructed. Plus, although it's priced separately from WordPress, if you hire a firm to build your site for you, they can likely have it added to your site as a part of their standard fee. That way, you get all of the amazing features of Elementor, now and down the line, without blowing your budget.

Recommended Website Design Services

Speaking of website design agencies, there's no shame in having someone else build your site for you! I've covered a ton of reasons and tools for doing it yourself, but not everyone has the patience and time to learn the process of building a website. Additionally, a web designer can bring a fresh perspective to your brand.

Outlining A Content Strategy

The final piece of the puzzle, when planning to market yourself as a speaker, is content. This includes blog posts, articles – all of the publications that showcase your experience as a speaker and your credibility in your target industry. Besides making you a better writer with time, there are plenty of benefits that come from writing content. I'm talking about increased traffic to your website, high-quality educational content for you to share on your social media profiles – everything I covered in the last section when it came to SEO.

But, how do you make the most of your content, when beginning to market yourself as a speaker? I'm not going to lie. It's not easy managing a content strategy on top of the rest of your speaking business. Throw in traveling from one speaking gig to another, and to say you have your hands full becomes an understatement. Luckily, next, I'll walk through all of the tips to quickly and easily get started.

The Basics of Keyword Research

To begin, before writing a blog or creating a video, it's important to verify your topic is useful. As a speaker, one of the amazing impacts you have is inspiring people from the stage. In the same way, choosing effective topics to write about allows you to do so from home. These topics are called "keywords" or "key phrases" and you use them every time you use a search engine, whether you know it or not.

For example, if you search "speakerflow" in Google, several results show up, including my website, YouTube channel, and social accounts. In this case, the keyword is "speakerflow" and each result has been designed to use that keyword regularly. Because of this, when you search for that keyword, Google's algorithm recognizes all of my pages that use it, making them show up in the list of search results. Makes sense, right?

Similarly, when you're looking for keywords, the easiest way to start is a simple Google search. Choose a keyword or phrase that you want to use when you market yourself as a speaker. A few examples of this are "generational speaker" or "leadership speaker". After you've searched for a keyword, scroll to the bottom and look for the "Searches related to" section. Here, everything listed is another keyword you could rank for, on your blog, a landing page, anywhere online.

Admittedly, this is a bit oversimplified, and there are a handful of tricks to make keyword research simple and stress-free

KEY FEATURES OF A GOOD YOUTUBE STRATEGY

After you've identified keywords, it's time to put them into action. One of the ways to do this is through You-Tube videos. Since Google acquired YouTube in 2006, videos have not only become more accessible. They've also been prioritized by search engines because of their engaging nature. As a speaker, this provides you with some unique advantages. To begin with, you're likely comfortable in front of people, so recording a presentation should be a piece of cake. Additionally, with keyword research, you're also aware of the things people are searching for. Essentially, a good YouTube video combines both of these things. Using them, you can find people searching for your message and then reel them in with your killer stage presence.

To create a solid YouTube video, there are a few important things to include so your video is SEO optimized. First, include your keyword in the title of your video. That way, when people search for your keyword, they'll see your video at the top of the list. They'll also see that the title uses exactly what they're looking for, making them more likely to click. Likewise, the second major component of a good YouTube video is using the keyword in the video itself. I know this seems common sense, but you'd be surprised how many people forget about it. Finally, don't skimp on the thumbnail for your video. Just like images in social posts, the more eye-catching your thumbnail, the more likely someone will watch your video.

KEY FEATURES OF A GOOD BLOG POST

Alternatively, if you're more of a writer than a speaker, when offstage, another way to reach people is through blogs. Like SEO as a whole, writing blogs can be time-consuming and stressful depending on your comfort as a writer. However, blog-writing is also like SEO in its worth over time, especially in the speaking space. Want to show an event planner how knowledgeable you are in their industry? Need something to include in an advertisement for your website? A blog can do both of these things on top of boosting the authority of your website. Plus, they make great shareable content for your social media accounts. What's not to love about that?

When writing blogs, using them to market yourself as a speaker requires a few tactics up your sleeve. First and foremost, don't skimp on the length of your blog. Ideally, each blog should be at least 1,500 words, and your keyword should make up 1-2% of those. Second, to break up those words, SEO experts generally recommend including graphics or videos throughout your blog. On top of making it easier to digest the content of your blog, including visuals also makes it more memorable. Plus, readers can share your graphics, leading anyone who sees them right back to your website.

BUILDING A CONTENT CALENDAR

At this point, we've covered a ton of information in this guide. From social media to keyword research, we've covered the A-Z of how to market yourself as a speaker. That said, you might be wondering, "How am I going to stay on top of all of this?" Fortunately, that's where a content calendar comes in.

Before anything else, we at SpeakerFlow use our content calendar to store our list of keywords. That way, we can keep track of them and delegate them to different members of the team, if needed. We also use our content calendar for the "calendar" part. In the same way, as you use content to market yourself as a speaker, your content calendar is your mission control. When you're writing a blog, recording a YouTube video, or posting to social media, it's your checklist. Basically, if I mentioned it in this guide, you can organize it in your content calendar.

Paid Advertising vs. Search Engine Optimization

Besides using social media to market yourself as a speaker, there are two other stellar ways to bring traffic to your website: paid advertising and search engine optimization (SEO). Depending on your focus industry, your budget, and the size of your team, each of these options can be beneficial for your speaking business for different reasons. However, by understanding the pros and cons of paid advertising and SEO, you can effectively use both in the future, even if one option is out of the question right now.

PROS & CONS OF PAID ADVERTISING

On the flip side of paid advertising, search engine optimization (SEO) allows you to market yourself as a speaker free of charge. If you're new to SEO, in short, it involves designing your content and your website with keywords, key phrases, and layouts suited to search engines. For the most part, SEO focuses on optimization for Google searches, simply due to the volume of people that use Google. However, regardless of the platform you're using and the content you're designing, the benefits of high-quality SEO remain the same.

Additionally, once you've used advertising as a part of a long-term plan to market yourself as a speaker, the data you can gain from it is unmatched. From understanding which ads are attracting the most visitors to where those visitors are most active, you can learn a lot from advertising data. That said, when it comes to data, that's where some of the cons to paid advertising come in. For the most part, collecting that useful data takes anywhere from 3-6 months. Because of this, in order to effectively and sustainably start a paid advertising campaign, you have to be willing to spend that 3-6 months of ad spend knowing you won't see a return until month seven.

Recommendations

Taking all these things into account, as a general rule, I recommend paid advertising if you are an established speaker and have consistent predictable revenue from your speaking business. In other words, if your sales aren't consistent yet, put a pause on paid advertising until you have that well in hand.

PROS & CONS
OF SEO

On the flip side of paid advertising, search engine optimization (SEO) allows you to market yourself as a speaker free of charge. If you're new to SEO, in short, it involves designing your content and your website with keywords, key phrases, and layouts suited to search engines. Primarily, SEO focuses on optimization for Google searches, simply due to the volume of people that use Google. However, regardless of the platform you're using and the content you're designing, the benefits of high-quality SEO remain the same.

First and foremost, investing time in SEO consistently results in greater traffic to your site from intentful visitors. That means more site visits from more people considering you for their event. In essence, this happens because people are generally searching Google with a problem in mind, searching for a solution. Because of this, if your website or a page on your site is tailored to appear on the first page of search engine results, they're more likely to see that you are the solution, and they need to hire you to help solve their problem. Sounds pretty great, right?

The bad news comes, again, in terms of time. Like paid advertising, SEO doesn't immediately produce results, even if you're investing a ton of time and energy in it. In fact, as a rule, it takes a minimum of six months to see traction in your SEO strategy and up to 18 months for a blog to fully actualize. In other words, even after you write a blog with keywords your audience is searching for (we'll talk about this shortly), your blog won't show up on Google right away. This is part of the reason that, in many industries, marketers are saying not to bother with SEO, even though you definitely should!

Recommendations

Admittedly, investing time in a solid SEO strategy takes diligence and consistency. However, the traffic your website will gain as a result of SEO remains consistent and predictable after those initial 18 months, making it well worth the time and effort regardless of the size or age of your speaking business.

When you market yourself as a speaker and focus on SEO, the same level of traction is possible in your speaking business

GETTING A SPEAKING GIGS

Advertising by word of mouth is beneficial because it's free and it creates a network of connections with all the people you inform about your speaking gigs. In addition to networking, you may need to apply for time slots at conventions, conferences, workshops and other venues. Research speakers who cover subjects similar to yours and find out where they speak. Get the names of event organizers and contact speaker bureaus to help you find high-paying engagements.

ace it – Tony Robbins didn't become "Tony Robbins" overnight. He was a nobody at some point in his life.

And if you're not a "nobody," then great! But if you are, don't fret. You can become a "somebody," but you might need to do speaking gigs for free at first. Once you gain a reputation, then people will want to pay you for your services.

Preparing to Book Speaking Gigs
Before you pick up the phone or draft an email, there's one important step that cannot be skipped: preparation. Preparing your materials and your message is of the utmost importance, especially if you plan to conduct your sales virtually. This prep work allows you not only to appear skilled and accomplished as a speaker. It also demonstrates to event planners how easy the entire booking process will be for them. It may sound rudimentary, the fact remains that more people will hire

you if you have your sh*t together. Plain and simple.

Types of Speaking Gigs

So, what exactly do you need to prepare? First, let's talk about the types of speaking gigs for which you would be booked. There are four types of speeches total: informative, instructional, ceremonial, and persuasive.

Informative speeches are intended to present an idea or topic. They should focus on raising awareness rather than presenting an argument.

Instructional speeches are for teaching or describing a process (think lectures).

Ceremonial speeches can be seen at important events and include commencement speeches or the best man's toast at a wedding. These are, for the most part, much less frequent than informative, instructional, or persuasive speeches.

Last but not least, persuasive speeches are intended to persuade. Surprising, right?

Depending on the speech you are giving, you may need to have different materials prepared to demonstrate your skills. For example, if you are presenting an instructional speech, you should have visual aids as well as at least one video of a past instructional speech, to show your capabilities. However, for a ceremonial speech, you are much less likely to need visual aids prepared but equally likely to need your credentials outlined.

Sales Materials to Prepare

That said, there are five pieces of your sales process that are absolutely critical, regardless of the type of speech. From your pitch to an event planner to the equipment you need, the more you have prepared, the better your chances of getting booked in the first place.

Speaker Website

The first piece of the puzzle for selling your speaking services is a fairly obvious one: your speaker website. Now more than ever, your digital presence can make or break your first impression, when you're considered for speaking gigs. Because of that, it's important that your website showcases your credentials, your speaking skills, and how to contact you.

Your website should also meet a few requirements, from a marketing standpoint, if it is up-to-date. These include optimization for speed, a simple and clear navigation bar, and simple animations (just to keep things engaging). Perhaps most importantly, your brand should be consistent throughout the various pages on your website. Everything from wording on the homepage to your brand colors is representative of your message, directly or indirectly. As a result, mindfulness for these parts of your website, while tedious, is guaranteed to pay off.

Social Media Channels

Next on your list of speaking materials to prepare is your social media. The three most common social media platforms used by speakers are Facebook, Twitter, and Instagram. First and foremost, these sites are demonstrations of your message and your engagement. After all, what shows your ability to engage people more than a long list of people that follow you online long after the gig ends?

If you don't already have business Facebook, Twitter, and Instagram accounts, now is the time to create them. By engaging with people on social media you connect with past audience members and continue to share your message. Additionally, from a sales standpoint, you demonstrate that your speech was engaging enough to captivate audiences even after it ended. In other words, you show event planners how amazing you are and that they should hire you again (or hire you in the first place).

At this point, you might be thinking, "Social media sounds great, but I don't have time to manage three or four social accounts," and you're 100% right. To solve the time-crunch conundrum (we all know it too well), enter social schedulers. I've actually mentioned a few of these already, such as Hootsuite and Later, but there are plenty of other options out there to help you automate posts to your social channels.

LinkedIn Profile

Now, there was one social media platform that we didn't mention, and don't worry. We didn't forget LinkedIn. Recently, LinkedIn has rapidly been growing into a place to connect with other speakers and prospective clients. This is true for a number of reasons. First, LinkedIn is first and foremost a professional community so it is more easy to narrow people down by their profession (such as event planners). Second, it's also easy for others to find you, as your LinkedIn profile can function as a digital resume. Finally, the publishing platform on LinkedIn is only getting bigger. As you're working to grow your online presence, each of these features are key things to keep in mind.

Digital Collateral

Moving on from social media, the next set of things to prepare probably comes as no surprise. These odds and ends make up the digital collateral collection that you provide to event planners once they book you. As with the other preparation pieces mentioned, having these materials perfected prior to selling shows your organization and the ease with which people can work with you. Below are the top five items I recommend preparing:

- Speaker One-Sheet
- Branding Kit (including your logo and brand colors)
- Headshots
- Biography (a long and a short version)
- Audio/Sound Requirements

Earlier, I mentioned speaker Jacob Green's site as an example of what an ideal site should look like. However, it's also a perfect example of these items. Specifically, his "For Event Planners" page is exemplary, as it outlines each of the bullets above among other details. In creating this summary for event planners, Jacob makes it easy for them to see his preparedness, consider his requirements, and make a decision in a matter of minutes. That's your goal, when you begin reaching out to event planners, too. Show them your worth with as little time and energy as possible, on your end and theirs. That way, they can get back to organizing the event and you can get back to speaking.

Speaking Fee

Finally, the last and perhaps the most important thing you should prepare is your speaking fee. No one loves having the "money conversation," but, by outlining your highest and lowest fees ahead of time, you better prepare yourself for it. Then, when it begins, you don't fall into the tiny-budget trap. This happens when an event planner, after hearing your fee, tells you, "Well, our budget is only half of that". Then, you say, "Okay, that would be fine"

Absolutely not! Prepare your fee ahead of time along with a list of past clients (who would testify that you are worth that fee). Then, stand your ground when the sales begin. Be sure to also know where you stand on expenses. If an organization's refusal to cover travel costs is a deal-breaker, make sure you know your bottom line beforehand, so you aren't caught off guard.

Besides having difficulty selling, most professional speakers also under-sell themselves. Namely, they don't know how much to charge for speaking gigs and so ask on the monetarily low side. So, before we go any further, you are likely worth more than you are charging, so plan some new prices! After all, it never hurts to ask.

The Basics of How to Book Your Own Speaking Gigs
Now that you have your website, social accounts, and

back-end materials prepared, let's move on to the main event: how to book speaking gigs. In this section, we'll take a quick look at the basics of speaker sales and how to avoid the most common mistakes. I'll also cover the top tech to bring into your sales process. From CRMs to document management, there are a host of tools we've used to maximize our sales process. Plus, after this, you'll be able to do the same!

Speaker Sales Collateral

If you've never sold before, it can seem intimidating to pick up the phone or send emails that focus solely on you. That said, rest assured that if we can do it, you can do it. To get started, sales as a professional speaker demands three things: preparation of your materials beforehand, knowledge of the event in question, and a thick skin in the face of rejection. The first of those things, preparation, includes not only the pre-sales materials we went over already. You should also have a process for handling leads, whether they are inbound or outbound, and standard templates for outreach to event planners.

The Basic Sales Process

Let's take a look at an example. The following speaker – let's call him Michael from Scranton – speaks about sexual harassment and time management in the workplace. Before selling, Michael makes sure that his website is updated and his digital collateral is prepared. He also writes an email template for event planners, in case they don't answer his call. This template includes links to his website and LinkedIn profile, and a brief explanation of why he would be a valuable speaker at their event. He also drafts a pitch letter to the event planner, in case he is unable to reach them by email or phone.

Finally, he researches the company that is hosting the event so that he knows the name of the event planner and the background on where and why the company is hosting the event in the first place. All in all, the process looks something like the image on the right.

Although Michael isn't real, this process is a basic outline of how most speakers can start selling with little or no experience. The key is to contact the event planner in multiple ways until he or she gives you a "Let's talk more" or "I'm not interested". This is where the last part of selling comes in: having a thick skin. If an event planner isn't answering your calls, emails, or letters, send another one. If they reject you for this year's speaking gig, ask about the gig for next year. It may be a little easier said than done, but don't get discouraged by a few "No"s or ignored emails. Booking speaking gigs, like any type of sales, is a numbers game, so the more event planners you reach and the more selling practice you get, the more your success rate will grow.

Technology for Booking Your Own Speaking Gigs

That said, besides the email templates and processes you can use to book more gigs, don't forget about technology. From organizing your incoming leads to setting reminders to follow up, using the right technology can mean less work in the long run. Below are just a few of the tools that we recommend as well as how you, as a rookie or expert speaker, can use them.

Customer Relationship Management (CRMs)

You've probably heard of a customer relationship manager, or CRM, whether it was in the context of getting speaking gigs or not. If you haven't heard of it, a CRM is basically a one-stop shop for your sales and marketing processes. Within your CRM, you can organize your contacts and leads, set reminders to follow up with them, and track your correspondence with them as they turn from a lead to a client.

In short, regardless of industry, a CRM can be a lifesaver when it comes to tracking leads and securing potential revenue. In the speaking industry specifically, having a CRM means having all of your sales information in one place. Additionally, most CRM companies have evolved to become cloud-based systems with high-quality mobile apps, so you can continue managing leads even while you're the road to a speaking gig already in the books.

Proposal Software

But how about technology for after you've closed the gig? Introducing proposal software. There are countless options on the market for creating gorgeous proposals, including Bidsketch, Proposify, and PandaDoc. This software allows you to streamline your proposal process, complete with personalized branding and a portal for event planners to pay right through the proposal itself. All it takes is some initial setup, and future proposals can be generated, sent, and paid, all in just a few clicks.

Although it sounds minimal, use of a proposal creator – like all of these tools – is all about saving time. Looking back at Michael, our workplace harassment speaker, his proposal software comes into play immediately after he's booked a gig. If he sends a sales email on Monday, meets with that event planner on Thursday, and gets a "yes" from her on Friday, he can get a proposal to her Friday afternoon in a matter of minutes. From start to finish, it took less than a week for him to book the speaking gig. That sounds like a dream, right?

eSpeakers

Another major player in the speaking industry, when it comes to sales, is eSpeakers. Started in 1999 by Art Berg, CSP, CPAE, eSpeakers serves as a speaking gig powerhouse. With built-in automations, event management features, and a database of meeting planners, each account allows you to find leads and turn them into clients, all in one platform. In short, eSpeakers is a sort of combination event management platform and CRM.

it was built by speakers for speakers, so it was already created with you in mind.

On top of its usefulness for speakers, eSpeakers has been of growing importance for event planners. As planners search for speakers, saving time and finding a quality speaker within their budget is of the utmost importance.

That's where eSpeakers comes in. Because you are given an eSpeakers speaker profile with your account, you're automatically entered into the eSpeakers marketplace. This hub of thought leaders makes it easy for event planners to find you, contact you, and book you for their speaking gigs quickly and with confidence.

G Suite

While a lot of these tools may be new, this one is an oldie but a goodie: G Suite. If you haven't heard of G Suite, you've likely still used one of the apps included in the G Suite package, such as Google Drive, Google Docs, or Google Calendar. Each of these apps, along with a handful of others, is combined in a single purchase for business owners. By using G Suite, you have a network of applications and tools available to you through a single login for a low monthly fee. The image to the right showcases just a few of the ways you can use G Suite applications in your day to day processes for booking speaking gigs.

Considering it solely from an organizational standpoint, G Suite is a game-changer. Besides being able to share information among your team, it also simplifies communication with decision-makers. Remember the digital collateral I outlined earlier? Once you have that information compiled, you can store it in a Google Drive folder for "Speaking Gig Materials". You can then share the link to that folder with event planners, so they can access and download the files they need without having to contact you repeatedly prior to the event. Then, after the event is over, you can send them a Google Form to submit feedback for your performance.

1Password or Last Pass

Another awesome day-to-day tool is a password vault. These apps are designed to safely and securely store login information for your digital tools. That way, you don't have to try and remember each one when you sign in, or worse, use the same username and password for all of them. I know how easy and convenient that sounds, but take it from me – that's definitely not secure. Looking at the sister that hacked my Facebook page...

ADDITIONAL OPTIONS FOR FINDING SPEAKING GIGS

Besides conducting your own outbound sales, there are a handful of additional ways to reel in speaking gigs. These options can be your main sources of gigs in the future but, for the most part, they should be supplementary. Especially if you're a rookie speaker, many of these options should take a back burner compared to stabilizing your own sales process.

Speakers Bureaus

The most common place that speakers look to when they want more speaking gigs is speaking bureaus. Without question, bureaus can be a great source of referrals, especially if you are a well-established speaker and an expert in your industry. Premiere Speakers Bureau, for example, boasts names like Richard Branson and Mel Robbins in their roster. For these speakers, they are established enough that their speaking fees are doubtless five-figures on average. This is especially important because speakers bureaus operate in the same way that ISRs do, but on a larger scale. In short, bureau reps are given commission based off their sales. As a result, in many cases, this leads to greater promotion of expensive speakers, simply for the fact that a sale for one of them means more commission.

This leads me to a key point, regarding speakers bureaus: Don't chase them. Attract them. The more you focus on building a firm foundation for your speaking business, the more three things will happen. First, your sales skills and those of your ISR will improve (surprise, surprise). Second, you'll book more speaking gigs and more high-end clients. Third, as a result, you'll be able to charge more for speaking gigs. Combined, these three things will bring bureau representatives to your door, motivated to sell your services to event planners.

Personal Referrals

Another option for increased numbers of speaking gigs comes in the form of personal referrals. As with speakers bureaus, these should not be your primary source of gigs if you are a rookie speaker, but can undoubtedly become so once you are established. To increase the number of referrals, first, track the referral source for each speaking gig you win, as mentioned earlier. This allows you to see who is already referring you so you can offer them incentive to continue doing so. For example, if Dunder Mifflin paper company has referred you five gigs in the past year, you could offer their employees free copies of your book, as a thank you.

The other way to bring more referrals your way is simply by asking. After an event has concluded, contact the event planner and let them know they're free to share your information or hire you again. It seems common sense, but so many speakers miss this opportunity! By adding it into your sales workflow, you can make it a standard process.

Speakers Associations

The last of the common ways to bring in more speaking gigs is through speakers associations. In North America, the two largest speakers associations are the National Association of Professional Speakers (NSA) and the Canadian Association of Professional Speakers (CAPS). Associations like these can be exceptional ways to learn from fellow speakers and make connections that could eventually turn into referrals. Like speakers bureaus, they're also attractive places for event planners to look for speakers. However, unlike speakers bureaus or personal referrals, speakers associations are unlikely to ever produce the majority of the speaking gigs sent your way. This is largely because speakers associations are designed for connections and education for speakers, making it more about speakers and less about event planners.

All in all, speaking businesses cannot function without outbound sales efforts. From phone calls to letters to emails, reaching event planners and getting them to choose you for their speaking gigs can be a complex and tedious process. Hopefully, this provided from clarity surrounding speaker sales efforts and some tips and tricks to give your sales a boost.

WRITE A BOOK

Professional speakers command respect as well as significant fees to speak and share their knowledge at events like conferences, conventions, summits, forums and corporate meetings. How about you? If you really enjoy speaking to crowds and sharing what you know, then perhaps you should consider starting a second career as a public speaker too.

I often say to authors that speaking is a wonderful opportunity to pique the interest of new audiences and drum up support for your book. If you're comfortable enough putting yourself out there, then giving speeches, giving classes and giving interviews can all help you to promote your book and promote yourself as an author. But it can also work the other way around.

If you thrive in the spotlight, then writing a book can help you to launch a whole new career as a professional speaker. Let me show you what I mean.

Writing a Book Opens Doors

Writing a nonfiction book fundamentally requires three things from the author: knowledge, research and passion. After all, nonfiction books are considered to be works of nonfiction because of the author's good faith effort to stick to accuracy and facts; it doesn't matter if we're talking about cookery, science or politics. Then passion is the main factor in being able to take a book project from initial idea to a complete, finished book that you can hold in your hands.

If you didn't have anything to say or didn't know enough about the subject of your book, or had enough motivation and discipline to write, you simply couldn't write a book. (Not without the help of a ghostwriter's services anyway.)

Writing a book is a testament to your knowledge of the subject and your commitment to it. That is why writing a nonfiction book bestows a level of credibility upon the author that can be hard to find elsewhere; it firmly establishes the author as an expert. And who do people want to come speak to their group or event? Why an expert, of course!

Writing a book can open doors to bigger and better things, and bigger spotlights. Many entrepreneurs, for example, use their books as part of their sales funnel for lead generation (to make more money). Their readers get access to that person's expertise in book form for the price of one or two cups of coffee. Then those wanting more are primed to pay for additional higher-priced services like consulting.

The same is true for speakers. A book can serve as both a ticket of admission to the speaking world (establishing your credibility), as well as a calling card (helping to lay the groundwork for a speaking engagement). In fact, this works even if the person booking speaking engagements doesn't actually have the time to read your book. Having written a book is enough to be your superhero cloak

How to Write a Book
For many people, writing a book has been a lifelong dream, yet one that's always seemed just out of reach.

Indeed, as I reveal in my publishing podcast Bestseller, roughly 80% of Americans have wanted to write and publish a book at some point — but fewer than 0.1% have actually done it.

So what's the secret formula that will unlock your creativity and show you how to write a book that will make your dreams come true? Some authors would tell you that there is no single path to authorship, as every writer's journey is unique.

We'd counter with this: almost every bestselling author will have highly effective writing patterns and habits that help them reach their goals. If you want to write a book of your very own, all you have to do is emulate them!

1. Find your "big idea"

The one thing you absolutely need to write a book is, of course, an idea. If you don't have that, you'll never get past the first page of your draft.

You may already know what you want to write about, or you may be at a total loss. Either way, you can settle on a "big book idea" by asking yourself a few simple questions:

- What do I want to write about?
- What do I feel is important to write about?
- Who will want to read about this story/subject?
- Will I be able to carry out this idea effectively?

Your answers to these questions will help you narrow

it down to your best options. For example, if you have several different ideas for a book, but only one that you're truly passionate about and feel you can pull off, then voilà — there's your premise!

On the other hand, if you lack ideas, these questions should steer you in a firmer direction. Think about the kinds of books you love to read, as well as books that have made a significant impact on you. In all likelihood, you'll want to write a book in a similar vein.

Tools to help you find an idea

If you're really grasping at straws, consider using creative writing prompts or even a plot generator to get the ball rolling! You might stumble upon an interesting concept or story element that sparks a "big idea" for your book. (And if you're still uninspired even after trying these tools, you may want to reconsider whether you really want to write a book after all.)

2. Research your genre

Once you've found your big idea, the next step is to research your genre. Again, if you're writing the sort of book you like to read, you already have a leg up! Reading books in your genre is by far the best way to learn how to write in that genre yourself.

But if not, you'll want to select a couple of representative titles and analyze them. How long are they and how many chapters do they have? What does the story structure look like? What are the major themes? Perhaps most importantly, do you think you can produce a book with similar elements?

Find out what people are reading

You should also conduct market research on Amazon to determine the most popular books in your genre. If you want your book to succeed, you'll have to contend with these bestsellers. Go to the Amazon Best Sellers page and find your genre in the lefthand sidebar:

Then read those books' blurbs to figure out what really sells. What do they all have in common, and why might readers find them appealing? Does your book hold up to these standards?

Finally, think about how your book can offer something NEW. For example, if you're writing a psychological thriller, will there be a particularly sneaky unreliable narrator, or maybe a series of twists that the reader never sees coming? If you're writing a nonfiction book, do you have a unique take on the subject, or a particularly deep well of knowledge? And so on.

Going above and beyond is the only way to give your book a chance in today's hyper-competitive market. So don't skimp on the genre research, because this will tell you where the bar is and how you can surpass it.

3. Create an outline

If you want to write a great book, you need to outline it first. This is especially important if it's your first book, since you need a solid blueprint to rely on when you get stuck! (Because believe me, you will get stuck.)

So how do you go about creating that outline for your book? I actually have a whole other post on the subject, but here are the essentials:

Pick a format that works for you. There are so many different types of outlines: the free-flowing mind map, the rigorous chapter-and-scene outline, the character-based outline, and so on. If one approach doesn't work for you, try another! Any kind of plan is better than none.

Have a beginning, middle, and end. Way too many authors go into writing a book with a strong notion of how their story should start... yet their middle is murky and their ending, nonexistent. Take this time to flesh them out and connect them to one another. Remember: the best books have endings that feel "earned," so you should try to be building toward it from the start!

Consider your conflict points. Conflict is at the heart of any good book — it draws in the reader, conjures tension and emotion, and ultimately reflects the themes and/or message you want to convey. You don't have to know exactly where your conflict will manifest, but you should have a pretty good grasp of how it works throughout your book.

Get to know your characters. If you haven't done much character development yet, your outline is the perfect opportunity to do so. How will your characters interact in the story, and how will these interactions demonstrate who they are and what matters to them?

4. Start off strong

Let's get into the actual writing and make a dent in your first draft. One of the most important parts of writing a book is starting the story! It's no exaggeration to say your first few pages can make or break your book — if these pages aren't good enough, many readers will lose interest, possibly never returning to your book again.

First off, you need an opening hook that grabs the reader's attention and makes it impossible for them to look away. Take a look at the first lines of these hit best-sellers:

"Mr and Mrs Dursley, of number four, Privet Drive, were proud to say that they were perfectly normal, thank you very much." — Harry Potter and the Sorcerer's Stone

"Renowned curator Jacques Saunière staggered through the vaulted archway of the museum's Grand Gallery." — The Da Vinci Code

All of these books fall into different genres, yet all their opening lines do the same thing: capture the reader's attention. You can imitate them by making a similarly strong, slightly furtive statement in your opener!

From there, your job is to maintain the reader's interest by heightening the stakes and inciting the plot. You should also make the reader care about the main characters by giving them distinct personalities and motivations. (Note that "main" is a key descriptor here; never introduce more than a couple of characters at a time!)

Of course, there are infinite ways to write your first chapter. You might have to experiment with lots of different opening lines, even opening scenes, to find the right balance — but it's worth the effort to set the stage perfectly.

5. Focus on substance

Many writers believe that the key to writing an amazing book is style: impressive vocabulary, elaborate sentences, figurative language that would make Shakespeare swoon.

We're here to dissuade you of that notion. While style is great (as long as your prose doesn't start to become purple), substance is far more important when writing a book — hence why you should focus primarily on your plot, characters, conflict(s), and themes.

Make sure your book is all killer, no filler

Of course, that's easier said than done, especially once you've already started writing. When you get to a patchily outlined section, it's tempting to keep writing and fill out the page with literary gymnastics. But that's exactly what this content is: filler. And if you have too much of it, readers will become frustrated and start to think you're pretentious.

This is another reason why outlining is so important. You need to KNOW your story in order to stay on track with it! But besides outlining, here are a few more tips for making substance a priority:

Every sentence must do one of two things — reveal character or advance the action. This advice comes straight from Kurt Vonnegut, and it's 100% true: if a sentence doesn't accomplish one or both of those things, try removing it. If the passage still makes sense, leave it out.

Be conscious of your pacing. Slow pacing is a symptom of excess description. If the events of your book seem to move like molasses, you're probably using too much style and not enough substance.

Use a writing tool to reduce flowery language. Speaking of great American novelists, Hemingway is a fantastic tool to help you write like the man himself! Simply paste your writing into the app and Hemingway will suggest ways to make your prose more concise and effective.

6. Write "reader-first"

Want to write a book that people will really enjoy (and buy)? Well, this is pretty much the cardinal rule: you should always be thinking about your audience and trying to write "reader-first."

For example, sometimes you'll have to write scenes that aren't very exciting, but that serve the overall story arc. Don't rush through these scenes just to get them over with! Even if they don't seem interesting to you, they contribute to the reader's experience by building tension and preserving the pacing — and the reader deserves to relish those things.

Create 'fake' people who will want to read your book

When considering your readership, you should also keep a proto-persona in mind for marketing purposes. These are constructed personalities that marketers use to better understand their target customers. The more your book can cater to this hypothetical reader, the easier it will be to sell!

Maybe you're writing a true-crime account for zealous true crime readers. Such readers will have pored over countless criminal cases before, so you need to include unique details to make your case stand out, and craft an extra-compelling narrative to engage them.

7. Set word count goals

Let's move on to practical ways that you can improve your writing habits. Word count goals play a huge part in creating an effective writing process, especially if you're trying to finish your book in a certain amount of time.

You should create word count goals for both your individual sessions and per week — or per month, if that's how you prefer to think about your writing output. For relatively novice writers, we'd recommend the following word count goals:

- 500-750 words per day
- 1,500-2,500 words per week
- 6,000-10,000 words per month

These goals are based on a pattern of 3-4 sessions per week, which is reasonable for a beginner, but still enough to make commendable progress. Even if you only follow my minimum recommendations — 500 words per session at 3 sessions per week — you can still easily finish your book in less than a year!

Speeding up the writing process

If you're looking for how to write a book as fast as possible, your word count goals should look a little more like this:

1,500-2,000 words per session

9,000-15,000 words per week

35,000-50,000 words per month

The figures above adhere roughly to NaNoWriMo, the event in which participants write an average of 1,667 words/day to complete a 50,000-word book in one month. It's hard work, but it's definitely possible to write a book that quickly; hundreds of thousands of people do so every year!

But as any author who's done NaNo can attest, it's also a pretty grueling experience. Most authors find it exhausting to write such great quantities for so many days in a row — and they still have to edit copiously once they're done.

If this is your first book, make sure you take your time, set manageable word goals, and gradually build to bigger goals... which is where our next tip comes in.

8. Set up a productive space

Another major component of how to write a book is where you write, hence why it gets a separate section. If you want to complete an entire book, you absolutely must find a calm, focused space for your writing.

This may be in your house, a coffee shop, a library, a co-working space — wherever you can work productively and without interruptions. It should also be a place that you can access easily and go often. Working from home is the most convenient option in this sense, but it may be difficult if you have family around, or if you don't have a designated "room of one's own" (i.e. an actual office, or at least a desk).

What does a good writing space look like?

Try out different locations to see what works for you. Indeed, you may find that you like to rotate writing spaces because it keeps you energetic and your writing fresh! But wherever you go, do your best to make the space:

Quiet (noise-canceling headphones can be very helpful)

Clean (no clutter, especially if you do chores to procrastinate)

Non-distracting (nothing too fun around to tempt you away from writing; turn off your phone so other people won't bother you)

Your own (cultivate a nice atmosphere in your home office with posters and plants, or simply take the same seat at your local café every time — truly carve out a "dedicated writing space")

9. Use writing software

We've already talked about a few different pieces of software to help you with writing a book. But if you haven't found the right app or program yet, never fear — there's plenty more where those came from!

Book writing software is a topic we've actually written an entire post about, but it's worth touching on a few of our favorite writing tools here:

Scrivener

Scrivener is the downloadable writing software of choice for many writers, and for good reason: it has an exceptional interface and tons of useful features. You can outline chapters with its drag-and-drop system, create labels for elements you want to track, and use various templates to plan AND format your book. If you want to feel like a true professional, you can't go wrong with Scrivener — and it's even free to try for 30 days.

Milanote

Or if you're not much for outlines because your thoughts are all over the place, Milanote can help. The super-flexible interface allows you to "mind map" just as you would longhand, and rearrange different sections as you please. When writing, you can see all your notes at once, so you don't have to stress about forgetting things. It's a very refreshing, intuitive way approach that's worth a try for all disorganized authors.

FocusWriter

Speaking of intuitive, what's more intuitive than simply writing on a piece of paper, no distractions — just like the old days? Meet FocusWriter, which allows you to do exactly that. The full-screen default interface is a sheet of paper on a wooden desk: no bells, no whistles, no distractions whatsoever. Seriously, this one will get you in the zone.

The Reedsy Book Editor

I couldn't leave out one of the coolest word processing, editing, and formatting tools on the market! All jokes aside, the RBE lets you cleanly format your book as you go, so you can watch it take shape in real-time. You can also add sections for front matter and back matter and invite collaborators to edit your text. Once you finish writing, you can export the files of your book.

10. Take setbacks as they come

Remember how we said you'd inevitably get stuck? Well, that's what this step is all about: what to do when you hit a wall. Whether it's a tricky plot hole, an onslaught of insecurity, or a simple lack of desire to write, all writers experience setbacks from time to time.

There are countless ways to overcome writer's block, from freewriting to working on your characters to taking a shower (yes, that's a legitimate tip!). However, here are some of the most effective techniques we've found:

Revisit your outline. This will jog your memory as to planned story elements you've forgotten — which may help you find the missing piece.

Try writing exercises. It's possible you just need to get the words flowing, and then you can jump get right back into your book. Luckily for you, we have a whole host of great writing exercises right here!

Share your experience with friends. This is another great role for your writing buddy to fill, but you can easily talk about writer's block with your non-writing friends, too. If you're struggling, it always helps to vent and bounce ideas off other people.

Take a short break to do something else. Yes, sometimes you need to step away from the keyboard and clear your head. But don't take more than a day or so, or else you'll lose momentum and motivation.

Most of all, remember to take setbacks in stride and not let them get you down. As platitudinous as that might sound, it's true: the only thing that can stop you from writing a book is if you, well, stop writing. So keep calm and carry on — every day brings new opportunity and you'll get through this.

11. Don't rush the ending

Ending a book is no easy task, and poor third-act plotting is one of the most common authorial pitfalls. (Cough cough, Stephen King.) Hopefully, you came up with a solid ending, or at least a few possibilities, back when you were outlining your book! But that won't prevent you from another ending-related peril: rushing through the ending.

The fact is, even if you've got a great ending for your book, you're going to be exhausted by the time you get there. You'll probably just want to dash it off and be done.

Resist the urge to do so! Just as your readers deserve thoughtful writing and consistent pacing throughout the story, they deserve the same here, even if it's almost over.

On that note, take your time with the ending. Again, ideally, you've been building to it this whole time; if not, consider how you might go back and add some foreshadowing. Try tacking on a few different endings to see which fits best. And if you're still at a loss, see what other people say about how your book should end.

12. Get tons of feedback

You can write all day, all night, to your heart's content... but if no one else likes what you've written, you might end up heartbroken instead. That's why it's crucial to request feedback on your book, starting early and from as many sources as possible.

Begin by asking your friends and fellow writers to read just a few chapters at a time. However, apply their suggestions not only to those chapters, but wherever relevant. For example, if one of your friends says, "[Character A] is acting weird in this scene," pay extra attention to that character to ensure you haven't misrepresented them anywhere else.

Once your book is finished, you're ready for some more intensive feedback. Consider getting a beta reader to review your entire book and provide their thoughts. You may want to hire an editor to give you professional feedback as well.

Finally, it might sound obvious, but we'll say it anyway for all you stubborn writers out there: feedback is useless if you don't actually listen to it. Separate yourself from your ego and don't take anything personally, because no one wants to offend you — they're just trying to help.

13. Publish your book

You've persevered to the end at last: brainstormed, outlined, and written a first draft that you've edited extensively (based on feedback, of course). Your book has taken its final form, and you couldn't be prouder. So what comes next?

Well, if you've taken our advice about catering to your target readers, you may as well give publishing a shot!

Now you're ready to finally, blissfully, thrillingly publish your book! You'll be glad to know that out of the entire publishing operation, this part is one of the easiest. Amazon and other retailers take you through the upload process step-by-step, and as long as you have your materials prepared, you should have no trouble at all. Here's what you can expect to do, in order:

- Enter your title and metadata

- Upload your manuscript file (MOBI for Amazon, EPUB everywhere else)
- Add your book cover (JPG, TIFF, or PDF)
- Price your book and hit "publish"!

Pricing is another decision that every author must make for themselves. That said, if this is your first book and your main goal is to gain recognition, you should price your book pretty low — between $2.99 and $5.99 to start. You can also run price promotions to make your book even cheaper, or free, for a limited time, which can be a huge boon to your downloads!

Should I publish outside Amazon?

Another big question when it comes to publishing: should I only pursue Amazon self-publishing, or "go wide" with other stores like Apple Books, Barnes & Noble, and Kobo?

For first-time authors, going Amazon-exclusive is often the best option, simply because it offers so much in return. Amazon-exclusive KDP Select allows you to run those price promotions we mentioned and add your book to the Kindle Unlimited library, where more readers can find it.

However, cutting out other platforms may be to your disadvantage if you live in an area where Amazon isn't quite so monopolistic, like Canada or Germany. It's also not great if you plan on making your book "perma-free," since Amazon only allows limited-time free promotions, or if you don't think your book will get many readers through Kindle Unlimited.

Bottom line: do your research and figure out what's right for you

LEVERAGE ON THE POWER OF PODCAST

While every armchair broadcaster with a voice-recording app is eager to get in the game, creating a professional-sounding podcast isn't as simple as that. This guide will tell you how to create, record and publish your own basic podcast—and get people to listen.

Before you start, be ready to commit

Before you rush into things, it's important to keep in mind that podcasts take a lot of effort to get going. It's easy to assume they are easy to produce because most are audio only, but don't be fooled. They can take a lot of time to put together, especially when you're first starting out.

Also, podcasts do best when they're released consistently. If you're interested in developing any kind of listener base, you have to be ready to release episodes on a regular basis. Podcasting can be fun work, but it's still work, and should be treated as such.

Don't expect to get rich from podcasting. It's possible to generate income from podcasting, but that usually requires advertisements and sponsorships and patrons —all of which you can get only after you've built up a listenership big enough to make it worthwhile to advertisers.

If you're not interested in starting a podcast for the fun

of it, or just to have your voice heard, you might not get much out of it unless you already have an eager audience.

The gear you'll need to get started podcasting

You can't start a podcast without equipment, and good equipment will go a long way. Here's what you'll need:

Microphone(s): Any microphone will work for recording your podcast, but listeners can usually tell the difference between low- and high-quality microphones. (I use four analog Audio-Technica AT2020s for my own podcast). As you shop around, you'll also need to decide whether you want to use a USB or analog (XLR) microphone. USB mics convert analog sound into digital, so you can plug a USB mic directly into any computer and start recording without much hassle, but you could potentially get lower audio quality compared to analog. Considering you don't need any extra tools or devices to record with a USB mic, they can be a little cheaper in the long run.

Analog microphones use XLR connectors, which means you need another device to get your audio onto your computer, but you can get higher audio quality and can use them with other sound equipment (if you had a PA system or wanted to play live music, for example).

Of course, if you have a gaming headset or other basic microphone around, you can easily use that to podcast, too, so long as the quality is decent. That won't work well if you are co-hosting or plan to have frequent guests, as you'll need multiple microphones to capture everyone.

Portable XLR recorder (optional): If you plan on using analog microphones for your podcast, you'll need something that captures your analog audio and converts it to digital. Portable XLR recorders can capture multiple microphone channels and allow you to do basic sound level adjusting and muting on the fly. Your Audio files automatically get organized and stored on a memory card that you can insert into a card reader or slot in your computer.

These are amazing tools, but they can be expensive. You can find them for anywhere between $100 and $500, depending on how many channels and options you need.

Audio interface (optional): If you want to record directly to your computer with your analog microphones, you'll need an audio interface. These devices allow you to plug in one or more analog microphones and will convert the analog audio to digital. Most audio interfaces will connect to your computer via USB or USB-C. Audio interfaces can cost as little as $30 and go as high as $300, depending on what you need.

A computer: Any Windows or Mac computer should work fine to record, edit and upload your podcast. Thankfully, editing audio doesn't take a ton of computing power. Additionally, depending on how you choose to record—directly to the computer or onto a dedicated recording device—your computer will also need the right ports. USB microphones, for example, will obviously need an open USB port. If you're using analog microphones with a portable XLR recorder or audio interface device, you'll need either a 3.5 mm audio-in jack, a USB/USB-C port, or in some cases, a FireWire port. Before you spend any money on equipment, make sure you have a computer that can support it.

Audio editing software: For the actual recording and editing, you'll need a Digital Audio Workstation (or DAW). There are a lot of good options out there, but the licenses for most aren't free. Professional-level DAWs like Reason cost anywhere from $99 to $599 depending on the features you want, while Pro Tools runs $29-$79 per year. Hindenburg offers audio editing software licenses for $95-$500, Reaper is a fully loaded audio production app that'll run you $60 and Adobe's audio editing software Audition CC is available with a $20.99 monthly subscription.

You probably shouldn't start dumping money into podcasting software as a beginner. Because of that, most people will recommend free open-source programs like Audacity when you're just getting started, and that's what we'll use an example throughout this guide.

Pop filters (optional): The clearer your audio can sound, the better. Pop filters, while not required, are fairly cheap and can keep your plosives from making a nasty sound on your recording. If you don't want to buy any, it's easy to make some of your own.

You might be thinking that all this equipment is pretty pricey, and you're not wrong. However, keep in mind that decent audio equipment will last forever if you take care of it. It may be expensive at the outset, but after the initial purchase, you're set.

Narrow your topic and find your niche

There are a ton of podcasts out there, which means that you can probably find a podcast about everything under the sun already. Don't get discouraged! While nearly every broad topic is already covered, you just have to find your spin on things to make an old idea something new.

For example, if you wanted to make a podcast about music, ask yourself if there's an audience out there for what you want to talk about. Maybe you narrow your idea down from music in general to bluegrass specifically. Now your coverage is specific: the music, people, and culture of bluegrass.

Once you have your topic narrowed down, it helps to add a spin to it. Maybe you talk about bluegrass music and culture while sipping moonshine with your co-hosts. It's kind of true that everything has been done before, but it hasn't all been done the way you would do it. Find an angle that's interesting and engaging—the more your passion shines through your podcast, the more people are likely to keep listening.

Download, install, and set up Audacity

As mentioned earlier, Audacity is a great DAW for podcasting beginners. It's open source, free to use as long as you like, and is available for Windows, macOS, and Linux.

Before you can jump into recording, there are a few tricks to getting it all set up properly:

- Download and install Audacity 2.4.1.
- Connect your microphone and open Audacity.
- See if your microphone is being recognized by Audacity by checking the drop-down menu next to the small microphone icon. If you see your mic, go ahead and select it.
- In the top-left corner, you should see the pause, play, stop, skip back, skip forward, and record buttons. Click the record button and talk into your mic to make sure it's working properly.
- Stop recording and playback what you just recorded to make sure everything sounds okay.
- Note that previously you had to download the LAME MP3 encoder to export your file as an MP3. LAME is now built into Audacity for Windows and Mac.

Record and edit your podcast in Audacity

Recording is pretty straightforward in Audacity, but there are a few things you should do before you jump into your first show:

Connect your microphone and make a quick recording the same way as before to check your audio levels.

You can adjust your recording volume with the slider right above the drop-down menu where you selected your recording device.

When you've found a good level, go ahead and remove your recording test by clicking the small X at the top left of the track. You don't need it anymore.

Make sure your recording space is silent and record

around 5 seconds of "silence." This is called room tone, and you can use this to cover up background noise while you're recording the real deal. You can mute this track for now by clicking the mute toggle button on the left side of the track. You can also minimize it by clicking the arrow at the bottom-left of the track.

Go to File > Save Project > Save Project As, and choose a name for your project. Keep in mind that this doesn't export any audio, just saves your progress.

Now you're ready to actually record the main part of your podcast. Hit the record button, and Audacity will start capturing your audio in a new track. When you're done recording, hit the stop button. It's as simple as that. Before you continue, be sure to save your work.

How to add intro and outro music

Writing and recording your own theme music is incredibly difficult if you don't know what you're doing (and it probably won't sound very good). Leave it up to the pros and find free tunes at any site that offers music under an Attribution International License or Attribution-NonCommercial International License—like the Free Music Archive:

- Browse the music by genre or via search.
- Find a track that you like and click the down arrow to download it.
- It might take a while to find exactly what you want, but when you do, all you have to do is credit the creator in your podcast description.

Now it's time to add music and make any necessary edits:

Go to File > Import > Audio. Locate any music you want to use within your podcast, and click Open. The music will get dropped into Audacity as its own separate track.

Find the Selection Tool in the Audacity toolbar. (It looks like a typing cursor.)

Drag the Selection Tool over the section of music you'd like to use for your intro and outro music.

With that section of music currently selected, find the Trim Audio button on the Audacity toolbar and click it. You should be left with only the section of music you chose.

While that section of music is still selected, find the Copy button on the toolbar and click it (you can also use CTRL+C or Command+C).

On the same music track, click anywhere to the right of that music section. Then find the Paste button on the toolbar and click it (or CTRL+V or Command+V). You now have your intro and outro music, but it's still not quite ready.

With the Selection Tool, select one of the music copies. Then go to Effect at the top and choose Fade Out. Do the same for the other music copy, but choose Fade In instead. Your intro and outro music is now ready to go.

How to edit out certain bits of audio in your podcast recording

If you need to cut something out of your podcast—like

swearing, if you're trying to keep clean, or information that shouldn't be made public—it's easy to fix:

Find the section of audio that you need to cut.

Use the Selection Tool and highlight the entire section you want to remove.

Find the Cut button on the toolbar and click. Boom, it's gone. (Alternatively, you could also use the Silence button.)

Remember the room tone you recorded earlier? You can copy a section of that and overlap it with the cut portion so you have a less-jarring silence.

With your music ready to go and your necessary edits made, you can now line everything up with the Time Shift Tool (two arrows connected by a thin line). Just slide each piece of audio in its respective track until you're happy with how all of the audio lines up. You might need to play around with it a little to find the sweet spot.

What if my podcast sounds bad?
If you feel like your audio isn't sounding as good as you'd like, there are few things you can tweak. For example, you can use Audacity's compression and EQ settings to get things sounding closer to radio quality.

Pick a strong name and create a cover art image
When it comes to people finding your podcast, the name you choose for it is important. John Lee Dumas, the host of the Entrepreneur on Fire podcast, suggests you pick a

name that communicates to your audience exactly what your podcast will be about.

If we return to the bluegrass and moonshine example, it could be something straightforward, like "Bluegrass n' Moonshine," or something less obvious, but still gets the point across, like "Sippin' and Singin': The Bluegrass Podcast." The title gives you an idea of the show's contents, but more importantly, your show would likely pop up in someone's search for podcasts about bluegrass music.

You'll also need an image for your podcast. This is the first thing people will see when they come across your show, so it should look good. An image is also required in order to list your podcast in directories like iTunes, Stitcher, and BluBrry, as well as podcast managers like Pocket Casts and DoggCatcher.

Cover art can be a photo or a piece of custom artwork, depending on how you want to represent your show. If the show is about you, you can even use a good photo of yourself. You can use a simple logo if you like, as long as it has something to do with what you talk about on the podcast. You want to make sure your image conveys what your show is really about as best it can.

No matter what you choose to use for cover art, make sure the show's title is on the image. If you're not comfortable making the image yourself, don't be afraid to hire a designer to do it for you from service-oriented websites like Fiverr or 99designs.

Podcast images need to be certain sizes as well, otherwise your artwork won't look as good when it's shrunken down. In fact, some directories won't even accept pod-cast feeds if your art isn't sized appropriately. Here's are the essentials you want to shoot for:

Image must be 1,400 x 1,400 pixels at minimum

Image must be in .jpg or .png format (.jpg preferred)

Image should look good—and readable—at 300 x 300 pixels

A good rule of thumb is to optimize your image for 150 x 150 pixels. If it looks good that small, you know you won't run into any problems. Daniel J. Lewis at The Auda-city to Podcast also recommends that you treat certain types of images differently so they always look their best:

For photo/image-based artwork, acquire the largest ver-sion possible and design within its dimensions.

For color- or illustration-based artwork, design in a vec-tor editor (like Adobe Illustrator) to make artwork that can scale to any size without losing quality.

You can do most of your image editing in Photoshop—or alternatives like GIMP and Pixelmator—with ease. When you have a good name and some decent art representing your show, you're just about ready to start recording.

Find a place to host your podcast
When you've finished tagging and exporting your pod-cast, it's time to find a place to host the MP3 file. Getting your podcast hosted is essential so you can start distri-buting your show to podcast directories and apps. Here are some of the best options for beginners:

SoundCloud: SoundCloud offers free podcast hosting (in addition to two competitive paid options for when you get a little more serious), and lets you distribute your podcast via RSS. Your podcasts will instantly publish to SoundCloud itself, which makes it really easy to share your podcast on social media, blogs, and other web sites.

Podbean: Podbean provides multiple tiers of hosting, including a free option (though the free hosting is fairly limited). The service has its own iOS and Android app for listening, as well as analytic tools, though you'll need to pay to get most of their best features.

Podomatic: Podomatic is super user-friendly. It offers free hosting with enough bandwidth and storage for podcast beginners. There's also a pro option that allows for more bandwidth, if you find that you like it.

Libsyn: Libsyn is one of the oldest dedicated podcast hosting sites and considered to be one of the best. Their lowest price plan is $5 a month with unlimited bandwidth—no free option, unfortunately.

Amazon S3: Amazon's hosting service offers a free plan, but it limits your storage (among other things). The paid service only charges you for the storage and bandwidth you actually use, meaning the cost can go up as your podcast grows in popularity.

Fireside: A newer podcast hosting platform from the creator of the 5by5 podcast network, Fireside offers unlimited storage, downloads, episodes, analytics, and a site for your podcast (with custom domain support) for $19 per month. Each additional podcast is an extra $8 per month. You can easily import your older podcasts from any valid podcast RSS feed in addition to other hosting sites including Soundcloud, Squarespace, and Libsyn. It also makes small details like chapter markers and metadata more accessible. If you've got a few episodes under your belt and want to provide a better experience for both yourself and your audience, try it out.

If you're new to podcasting, or hosting media files online in general, try out the free services to see if you like the way they work. When you find one you like, it's worth paying for hosting if you're serious about continuing your podcast. Each host listed here will provide you with easy-to-follow instructions for how to upload your podcast audio file, but there are some basic steps to follow no matter which service you choose:

When you sign up for the service, use the name of your podcast (or the closest thing to it).

Upload a cover art image that is at least 1,400 x 1,400 pixels.

Fill out all sections of your profile, especially your show's description.

Upload your MP3 file. Most hosting services let you listen to your podcast right within the site, so give it a listen to make sure everything sounds good.

The file's metadata that you created before should fill in a lot of the necessary information. However, if something doesn't look right, now is the chance to make changes and fix it before you submit your RSS feed to any directories.

Once you're happy with how everything looks, you're ready to validate your feed and submit it to podcast directories.

Get on Apple Podcasts

There are a lot of podcast directories out there that you can submit to, including Stitcher, Blubrry, and Miro. Most podcasters, however, will tell you that if there's only one directory you should try to get listed in, it's Apple Podcasts, because it's the most popular and has the largest reach. Here's how to get listed in the Apple Podcast directory:

Check your title, author, description, and cover art that's associated with your podcast audio file on your hosting service. Apple Podcasts uses those fields for search. For more information and tips, check out the official Apple Podcast specs here.

Locate your podcast RSS feed URL and copy it.

Make sure your podcast RSS feed is valid. Some hosts have a built-in validator and will say if your feed is valid. Otherwise, paste your feed URL into Cast Feed Validator and see what podcasting apps and directories will see. Make changes at the hosting site as necessary.

Sign into Podcasts Connect with your Apple ID. To get started, you'll have to test and validate your podcast by adding your RSS feed (click the "+" sign to add and hit "Validate").

Preview your podcast and fix any errors.

Once your RSS feed has been validated, you can submit

it for review to be published. Track your podcast's status on your Podcasts Connect dashboard.

That should do it! If you don't see anything pop up in Apple Podcasts right away, don't stress. It can take from 24 hours to two weeks before your podcast is added, as your podcast must first be reviewed by a team of people. Fortunately, the process of getting listed in other podcast directories isn't much different, so once you've got Apple Podcasts figured out, the sky's the limit.

Finally, as exciting as it is to get your podcast out there for everyone to hear, consider waiting to submit your first episode until you've already got a few of them in the can. Submitting only one episode can leave a lot to be desired for those that stumble upon your show. It's also less likely that you'll be featured or promoted as something new and noteworthy. So record three or four episodes before you start trying to grow your audience

HOW TO PROMOTE YOUR PUBLIC SPEAKING VIDEOS

If you are just getting started with your career as a public speaker, one of the best ways to promote yourself can be with good video footage.

If you are giving a lecture, presentation, talk, or any other kind of public speaking, especial at a large event, ask if your talk will be filmed. If your event planner has a great video team, make sure to ask them if you can use the videos they make to promote yourself.

Then, follow these steps to make sure that your video reaches as many people as possible.

Get your public speaking video on Youtube.

Your first tip is to make sure that your public speaking video is uploaded to youtube. Often your event organiser may have their own youtube channel, or you may want to start your own and upload the video to your own youtube page.

Youtube is by far the easiest way to share videos of your public speaking or your talk.

Youtube offers lots of settings that you can use to help improve your public speaking. For example, you can choose to turn comments on your video on or off. If you turn off your comments, it means no one can say nasty things about your talk. If you turn comments on, it means that you might be able to incorporate some of the comments from people into future versions of the talk.

If there is something unclear in your talk, something confusing, or incorrect information, people in the comments will let you know.

Remember if there are comments that are downright nasty, mean, offensive, or what you might consider as cyber-bullying, use YouTubes own "Report Abuse" functions

Youtube can give you several very important functions when you click on the "Share" button under your video.

The first function is it allows you (or anyone you know) to easily share your public speaking video across a variety of social media platforms. It also allows you to get a short link that you can send to anyone to see your public speaking in just one click. Finally, it has an "Embed" option, that allows you, or your webmaster, to place the video inside your own website.

Embed your public speaking video onto your own website.

Youtube makes this so easy to put your public speaking video onto your own website or blog.

By clicking "Share" and then "Embed" YouTube gives you special code that you can copy-and-paste directly into your own website, or your own blog, to make the video appear directly on your page.

At first, it may look a little technical, but it is really easy, and your web designer can get your public speaking video into your website in just a few minutes of work.

Youtube also has some great features for embedding your public speaking video into your website. You can chose when your video starts playing. This can be great if you want to "fast forward" through a long introduction by the events host. Or if the video is 5 hours long from an all-day event and your talk starts at the 3 hour mark, you can skip to the exact second your talk begins.

There are many other options you, or your web designer, can add to your embedded public speaking video, such as making the video play automatically, or changing how the controls for playing or pausing the video are displayed.

Add a link to your public speaking video in your email signature.

This is one of the easiest and fastest ways to promote your public speaking video online. Simply take the short link from youtube by clicking "Share" and then "Copy".

In your email software you can edit your email signature. This is the part of your email that typically contains your company information, phone number, and all the other stuff at the bottom of every email you send.

Here is the perfect place to add the link from YouTube to your latest public speaking video, perhaps with a little line of descriptive text saying "Click here to see my latest conference presentation"

This means that every time you send an email, another person gets to watch your latest talk.

Incorporate videos of your public speaking into your social media channels.

Make sure that your video of your public speaking is shared on channels like Facebook, Linked In, Twitter, and anything else you may use.

Make sure your videos are prominently promoted and easy to find.

Always set your videos of your public speaking to "Public" so that your friends can also share them. You may want to directly ask people "If you like my public speaking video, please share it with someone who may enjoy it". This can bring a lot of new viewers to your public speaking video.

Combine your public speaking videos with others, and share them.

A great way to promote videos of yourself public speaking is to make a blog post or article where you might collect several different talks by other public speakers, and put them together in a list.

You can use YouTube's embed codes for any video. Not just your own videos. And it's perfectly legal to share other peoples public speaking videos alongside your own.

You may want to think about what is special about you and your talk, and find several other videos that share a common theme, and put them all together in an article on your website.

For example, you might want to think about these ideas for inspiration:

My top 10 talks by female entrepreneurs.

The best 5 presentations by Danish Athletes.

Top lectures every Physics student should see.

The most inspiring public speaking by teenagers.

The best TED talks by teachers.

Whatever your subject is, find several other great speakers who have talked about similar topics, and put your talk alongside theirs in a playlist. Maybe adding a little bit of text under each video saying what you like about the talk.

THE BENEFITS OF A KEYNOTE MOTIVATIONAL SPEAKER

Keynote speakers make for fantastic entertainment at a wide range of events and have the ability to inspire, educate and motivate audiences.

Hiring the right keynote speaker can transform your event from an ordinary occasion to an event that will live long in the memory of everyone involved.

I have compiled a list of reasons as to why a keynote speaker can be beneficial for your next occasion.

Able To Engage Audiences

This is perhaps the most important thing a keynote speaker can do at an event. Irrespective of the topic of your occasion, you need to keep audiences interested and engaged throughout the evening otherwise you run the risk of people getting bored and leaving early.

Hiring the right keynote speaker can eliminate this danger as they can share stories with audiences regarding their own careers teaching people various skills that they can take on board in their own lives. An example of a keynote speaker we work with who always keeps audiences captivated is British futurist Ben Hammersley.

Having appeared on numerous television documentaries and performed keynote speeches at some of the most prestigious venues in the world on the topic of technology, digital innovation and social cultural trends always leaving people wanting more.

Inspire People To Be The Best

Many organizations hire keynote speakers to make a difference in their own work place, motivating people to be the best they can be, and go far in both their professional and personal lives. Encouraging people to work hard, never give up and be ambitious, a good key-note speaker will see people leaving their events keen to make changes for the better.

One of our expert keynote speakers who can help with this is successful business woman and entrepreneur Sarah Willingham. Famous for being a former Dragon on Dragon's Den, Sarah has managed high-profile High Street restaurants including Pizza Express in her career, inspiring success in a whole host of food establishments.

At all of her keynote speaking events, Sarah is able to demonstrate people how it is possible to be successful in all walks of life.

Overcome Adversity

Throughout everyone's careers there will be occasions when they have to confront negative experiences and overcome them. Whilst this is necessary if you are to be successful, it is easier said than done and this is where a keynote speaker can come in handy.

Able to teach people how to overcome this adversity, one of the keynote speakers who excels at every event they attend is Virgin owner and entrepreneur Sir Richard Branson.

From a young age it was clear that he would go far but he faced many hurdles on his way to success. Starting a record shop in the 70s, at the time there was several restrictions on selling products. Despite this, Sir Richard still believed in his business model and has gone on to build a billion-pound company.

CONCLUSION

Have you ever dreamed of being the next Martin Luther King (minus the tragedy) or Tony Robbins? Would you love to travel the globe speaking to, and inspiring, millions of people with your message?

If you answered yes, I am glad you took the time to read this book and I hope it helped give you some direction as well as answered some of your wquestions.

Even though you have the goal and the dream of being a motivational speaker, that doesn't mean that it's going to be easy to accomplish. It takes a lot of effort and dedication. It's not for the faint of heart.

It can be done, and YOU can do it! There are plenty of people in the world who make a living as a motivational speaker. So, why not you?

Becoming a motivational speaker doesn't happen overnight, but it can be a great way to earn a living or simply just to earn a few extra bucks.

The most important part of becoming a speaker is that you will be helping many people who need to hear your message as well as people who didn't know they needed to hear your message. What better way to leave your mark on this world than building your legacy through speaking your experiences and truth to the ears that need to hear.

As much as we put stock into the things we read about

online and through social media sources, the spoken word continues to transcend every generational gap and carries the most impact. We hear something, we tend to believe it more than what we read in text. This is why motivational speakers are getting more recognition nowadays, because of the "power" and influence that they wield with their words, and how they deliver them.

ABOUT THE AUTHOR

William "King" Hollis

William "King" Hollis is an international motivational speaker, author & coach. From being homeless to quickly becoming one of the top motivational speakers in the world, he has truly spoken his way to success. That same passion, authenticity and his unique  gift of connecting to the hearts of people everywhere led him to accomplish something no speaker has ever done. In 2019 he made history by becoming the first and only paid motivational speaker featured at the highly prestigious Fashion Week held in Milan, Italy. This proved to be a turning point and solidified him as being one of the greatest young motivational speakers of our time. From everyday listeners to celebrities, actors, professional athletes and leading corporations, his speeches continue to make him a household name in personal development. Over Four hundred million views on youtube, the number one high school football speech, and tens of thousands of subscribers later, he still continues to pursue his mission with a hunger for inspiring tomorrow's leaders within every community. Additionally, he has currently released his new book "The Best Gift Comes From The Bottom" which is quickly becoming a best seller and is now available in multiple languages through his website www.kinghollis.co

Made in the USA
Columbia, SC
11 November 2020

24342395R00095